The Step

THE STEP
One Woman's Journey to Finding her Own Happiness and Success
During the Apollo Space Program

Published in New York, New York, by Morgan James Publishing. Morgan James and The
Entrepreneurial Publisher are trademarks of Morgan James, LLC.
www.MorganJamesPublishing.com

The Morgan James Speakers Group can bring authors to your live event. For more
information or to book an event visit The Morgan James Speakers Group at
www.TheMorganJamesSpeakersGroup.com.

A **free** eBook edition is available
with the purchase of this print book.

CLEARLY PRINT YOUR NAME ABOVE IN UPPER CASE

Instructions to claim your free eBook edition:
1. Download the Shelfie app for Android or iOS
2. Write your name in **UPPER CASE** above
3. Use the Shelfie app to submit a photo
4. Download your eBook to any device

ISBN   9781630477141   paperback
ISBN   9781630477158   eBook
Library of Congress Control Number:
2015911909

Cover Design by:
Chris Treccani
www.3dogdesign.net

Interior Design by:
Chris Treccani
www.3dogdesign.net

In an effort to support local communities and raise awareness and funds, Morgan James Publishing
donates a percentage of all book sales for the life of each book to Habitat for Humanity Peninsula
and Greater Williamsburg.

Get involved today, visit
www.MorganJamesBuilds.com

Habitat
for Humanity®
Peninsula and
Greater Williamsburg
Building Partner

To: Denise,
Best Wishes
Martha Lemasters
'0/19/'16

THE
STEP

One Woman's Journey to Finding her Own Happiness and
Success During the Apollo Space Program

MARTHA LEMASTERS

NEW YORK

TO ALL THE HARD WORKING MEN AND WOMEN WHO
MADE UP THE LAUNCH SUPPORT TEAM AT KENNEDY
SPACE CENTER IN THE 60'S AND 70'S—AND TO MY THREE
WONDERFUL DAUGHTERS: CURRAN, CATHY AND CINDY;
AND TO MY LATE BROTHER, HERSCH GOODWIN, WHO
FIRST READ MY BOOK AND ENCOURAGED ME.

CONTENTS

PREFACE

Recently on a trip to Potomac, Maryland, the whole family, consisting of my three daughters, spouses and grandchildren, sat down to dinner at a huge table in a private room in one of the finer restaurants. My daughter, Cathy, had married a very nice Jewish lawyer and their youngest daughter, Eliza, would be celebrating her 13th birthday with all the joy and fun that the bat mitzvah ceremony promises.

We placed our orders and during the wait my grandson suggested we play a game. It consisted of going around the room and providing answers from questions that would be asked. Questions began with "which three persons, living or dead, would you like to invite to dinner?" Finally, the question was posed, "At which historical event would you have liked to have been present?"

Several interesting answers followed: Gettysburg Address, Columbus discovering America, the signing of the Declaration of Independence. When it came my turn, I said, "Well, I *was* present at the most significant historical event of the 20th century that America has ever witnessed…the Launch of Apollo 11…and the subsequent landing of men on the moon. I can think of no other place in history that I would trade for the opportunity I had to witness the excitement, dedication and teamwork that I experienced on the Apollo Program during those magnificent days."

I was a witness to the fact that there were heartaches, failures, divorces, losses, challenges to the individuals who made up the Apollo launch support team…those individuals who day by day, endured the pressure, the constant challenge to make it happen despite all the tribulations and difficulties.

The rise in the awareness and respect of a woman's role in business began in the 60's and the Cape was no exception. I advanced from the typing pool, to secretary, and finally, writer—a witness to all the majesty and scientific ingenuity America could produce.

NASA's Manned Flight Awareness Program stated it best: "Zero Tolerance"—perfection was expected. I'm going to tell you about, what I believe to be, one of the greatest technical teams ever assembled in American history. This book is about some of the everyday people who made up this team: the managers, the programmers, the systems analysts, the engineers, the secretaries and typists, the writers…the men and women who made up IBM's launch support team for Apollo. Yes…it's also about my metamorphosis from a naïve, sexually unsatisfied young woman to a successful one in every avenue.

How did these marvelous men and women who achieved so much get through it all? How did their families fare? What became of them when the Apollo Program ended?

This creative, non-fiction memoir is based on my actual experiences over a nine-year period. This memoir is historically correct; however, names have been changed, events compressed, characters combined, and some incidents have been changed to protect identities. Certain scenes are imaginative re-creations based on my recollections. This book is truthful in as much as I can remember after more than 45 years.

Go back with me to those days in the 60's and 70's—to learn about the chosen, handpicked IBM launch support team that lived and breathed the Apollo Program and made it all happen.

ACKNOWLEDGMENTS

My sincere appreciation to IBM and NASA for their assistance and permission for the photos, IBM Engineer Clancy Boswell, who helped me get the technical information right; Jim Handley, George Smith, my brother, Hersch Goodwin; my fellow IBM writer at the Cape, Joanne Lauterbach Miller, who tediously proofed this book; photographer Aric Attas; Richard Marx, Brewster Moseley, Kay von Weller, Laura Steward, my assistant Tori Blackhart, Darcie Rowan, and my editors at Morgan James Publishing: Jessica Foldberg, Margo Toulouse, Bethany Burt and Nickcole Watkins.

INTRODUCTION

often wonder about old southern tales, sayings and predictions. My mother and grandmother have plenty of them, doling them out to me as sacred gospel. Mrs. Spalding, my fifth grade teacher, recites them to our class occasionally. Are they true and should I believe in their predictions and efficacy?

It is a memory that I recall many times, for inspiration, for confidence, or to simply smile, sit back and remember…

The year is 1948 and I am eleven years old in the sixth grade at South Side Elementary School in Ft. Lauderdale. It's a warm sunny May day with the anticipation of the end of school in everyone's thoughts. At recess, I'm playing softball with the sixth grade girls against the fifth grade girls. I hit a long ball, a sure home run. I round the bases and jump on home plate, positive of my home run and jubilant with my efforts; my friends cheer me on as if I'm some famous softball player, only to be told the exact opposite.

"You're out!" yells my teacher, strict Mrs. Spaulding, who is refereeing the annual game, in her three-quarter-length dress and chunky black shoes, behind the plate.

"You failed to tag second base," is her decree.

"But, I must have touched second base."

"No, you went right by it. You have to touch every base."

I feel my chin rise, my teeth clinch, but I don't cry. I know I'll be up to bat again and know what I have to do and will do. The very next time at bat, I whack it even further than my first supposed home run. I traverse the bases, pouncing on every base with both feet, and once again I jump on home plate, looking up at Mrs. Spaulding, with both arms raised.

"Well done," she says.

Later, back in our classroom, after the school bell rings, signifying the end of the day and the end of the school year, I rise to leave with the rest of the class. Mrs. Spaulding says, "Martha, please stay after, I'd like to talk to you." I return to my desk and anxiously wait. Am I in trouble for my grandstanding? After the last students leave the room, she motions me to come to her desk.

"Since this is the last day you'll be in my class I want to tell you something," she begins in her slow southern accent. "I want you to tell your parents what I am going to say to you. Will you do that?"

"Yes Ma'am, Mrs. Spalding."

"You've not been the smartest child in my class. You're good at what you like to do, but there is another ingredient that you do have that will take you far in this world. You've got '*The Step*.' Your dogged determination is something that will stay with you and enable you to achieve."

She notices the confused look on my face, "Honey, '*The Step*' is an old Southern term. When you have a goal, your 'step' is concentrated and it hurries you along, guides you to win, or to accomplish. Your pace becomes a little faster; your stride is determined and strong, you become more focused."

She pauses, looks right into my eyes to see if I fully understand her message.

"You'll understand what '*The Step*' means some day," she says, " I mean its full meaning, the way it can transform and perform miracles."

. . . .

CHAPTER 1

GROWING UP IN FLORIDA

Maybe it's my parents, or going to Sunday school that instills in me a great urgency to never use the words, "I can't."

I grow up in the 40's and 50's in sunny Ft. Lauderdale, going barefoot most of my early years except for school and church. Every day from the age of 10, I am either on the tennis court or at the beach. I can still smell the ocean and feel the sand beneath my toes…the burnt smell of my skin from too much sun.

We kids walk or ride our bikes everywhere. We don't lock our doors either…how would our friends get in? No one in my family has ever owned an umbrella. If it rains we just run through it and get wet.

Nasty, annoying mosquitoes are rampant. In the summer, the highlight of every evening at twilight is the spray truck that rides through the neighborhood dispersing DDT to kill the mosquitoes. All the kids

My dad and mother, Herschell and Nellie, who never allowed her crippled hands to be photographed.

jump up, run out of the house into the dense fog of DDT as if it is some magic cloud.

My Dad, a tall, handsome, Georgia boy, owns an awning and canvas company, located in a building facing New River, maybe 50 steps from the bridge on Andrews Avenue. He is a humble man, of few words, unencumbered by a high sense of ego, who provides modestly for our family of five. I have one brother and one sister. My Dad not only sews awnings but is also a master craftsman, or so he says, for making beautiful sails for huge, expensive yachts.

One of his more memorable customers is the movie star, Errol Flynn. "After I finished loading his sails aboard his yacht, Flynn insisted that I come sailing with him so I can see my sails billowing in the wind. I had to tell him what I tell all my customers: Can't do it. I get seasick," he says to the family at the dinner table.

My mother, tall and apple shaped, works all day with her household duties. I don't know of any women my mother's age who work outside the home. My mother rules the roost and is the voice of the family. She is also a strict disciplinarian who makes us pick our own switches from the yard when the need arises.

"You can do anything you set your heart to do…you have intelligence… use it." She also refuses to allow us to complain. "Complaint is poverty… and we are not poor."

My mother has crippling, painful, rheumatoid arthritis that's left her hands and feet badly deformed. Still, she does all the work that is required of women of her day—cleaning, washing, ironing and cooking everything from scratch—while the children take over clean up duties in the kitchen following our meals. Those crooked hands sew and mend my clothes, and darn the holes in my Dad's socks.

She doesn't enable her deformity to give her permission to neglect us. Having grown up seeing her with badly malformed fingers and feet, I don't realize they're different from any other mother's hands until late in the sixth grade when Mary Lou Cunningham asks me what is wrong with my mother's hands. Then, the wonder of all she accomplishes hits me and I am amazed at my mother, in awe of her perseverance and determination. She is an inspiration. Because if she can accomplish so much and never complains, imagine what I can do with healthy hands and feet.

Mama takes to bed most days in the afternoons. Later, the arthritis develops in her knees and she is unable to walk except within the house. She misses all my school events: never sees me play tennis, or even graduate. Finding shoes that don't cause additional pain is also difficult. By junior high school I realize that my mother is in too much pain to care for another infant.

One day, Dad brings Mom home from a "doctor's visit" and I see blood running down her legs. She stays in bed for weeks, running a fever, my Dad looking after her. Our house is small, just two bedrooms, it's easy to hear my Dad talking to my Mom through the thin partitions. He is trying to sooth her tears as she tells him "I'm so sorry. I would have liked to have another child but I just can't do it. My fingers can't even open a safety pin. Please forgive me."

"Don't you bother asking forgiveness from me. I see your pain, and I feel it too. I know how painful every step is for you. I'm just sorry I couldn't afford to send you to a real doctor to have this done," he says holding her crippled hands in his. Later, Dad brings all the kids together in our small living room.

"Your Mom's real sick, kids, so I'll need you girls to take good care of her while I go to work," says Dad, as he directs his speech to me and my sister, Zola, since my younger brother is only in the first grade. "She's not going to be able to cook or wash your clothes so you've got to help out. You've got to fend for yourselves."

We make sandwiches for everyone for several days until my Dad can't take it anymore and appeals for help from my Mom's brother and his wife, Charles and Ethel. When they arrive we are treated to real food again, country fried steak, mashed potatoes with gravy and fresh vegetables, and clean sheets.

Another doctor is called to the house. I overhear him tell my Dad, "It doesn't look good. She's got a fifty-fifty chance of surviving. I can't put her in the hospital—she'll be arrested for having an illegal abortion. You'll just have to wait it out. That guy that performed this probably didn't use sterile instruments. Rich couples have access to good doctors that will perform this procedure if the money is right, so I understand your situation. I'll leave her some medicine. Good luck."

I realize the seriousness of my Mom's malady when she is unable to get up in the mornings to fix our breakfast. When questioned, she just asks us to pray for her. And we do. It takes several weeks but each day she rallies a little more until finally one morning she gets up, dresses and fixes breakfast for everyone.

My mother has only five spices in her kitchen: salt, pepper, mustard, ketchup, and Tabasco. Every Sunday we are treated to fried chicken, pole beans, mashed potatoes and her wonderful pies; lemon, chocolate meringue, or key-lime…and on special occasions Charlotte Russe, which has to be served in the footed cut-glass bowl that my grandmother has brought from Alabama.

In our backyard are avocado, mango and kumquat trees. My mother's idea of a salad is a sliced avocado with lemon juice on it. Her only other salad is a tomato, iceberg lettuce, onion and mayonnaise mixture, with lots of salt and pepper.

During the heat and humidity of the summers, right after dinner, we are loaded into the car and taken to the beach where we play in the surf until almost dark. Later, in our beds, with only a fan to cool us, we are so tired from swimming in the surf that we fall fast asleep, oblivious to the sweltering heat.

When I am old enough to learn to drive and earn my learners' permit, my Dad takes on the task of teaching me. He is not a man of great patience. He often yells, only to reinforce my inability to get the clutch in smoothly. When parking, he advises: "You must find shade. Those seat covers and even the steering wheel can get hot enough to burn your skin."

My grandmother, my mother's mother, also lives with us, sleeping on a rollaway bed in the living room at night. She and my mother's entire family come from Alabama. Granny, as we call her, has an old book entitled, *The Confederate Soldier*. It is similar to my school yearbook. It has all the names of the Confederate battles and the officers who commanded the troops. My grandmother's dad was an officer in the Confederacy so she spends many hours instructing her grandchildren about his courage and honor. She spends the rest of her time reading *Science and Health, with Key to the Scriptures*, by Mary Baker Eddy.

She always asks me where the young men are from when they come to the house for a date when I am older. If they are from the south, she wants to meet them and find out exactly where his family is from in the south. If he is a Yankee, she will not even come out of her room.

My Dad is equally entrenched in southern history and fills our vacations with trips to every Civil War battlefield and museum in the south.

My mother never fails to point out lone standing fireplaces, the only remnant left from a house fire, as evidence that Sherman has burned the house to the ground. For years afterwards, every time I see a lone fireplace I am sure Sherman has been there and burned down that house. According to my calculations his march extends much further than Atlanta to Savannah.

Dad, cigar hanging from one side of his mouth, plaid shirt with his tie tucked in-between the buttons, cuts down a pine scrub for our Christmas tree and we decorate it with tinfoil and popcorn. My mother, with her bright apron on, fixes the traditional Southern meal: turkey, cornbread dressing and giblet gravy with boiled eggs, sweet potato pie, pole beans...and always a Claxton, Georgia fruitcake that Aunt Lila sends us.

By high school I have blossomed into a 5 foot 8 inch, well shaped brunette with killer legs. My mother thinks I'm too much of a tomboy. She sends me to a charm school where I learn to correctly walk and hold myself. I even win a contest for "Miss Leg Perfection." I enjoy high school, have lots of friends, make better than average grades, play on the tennis team...have one boyfriend throughout the last two years. I excel in English and writing and put my writing talents to work on the school newspaper and yearbook. I even quarterback the junior girls to a first-time victory over the seniors in flag football. The latter provides my Dad's favorite photo of me, as the guys from the football team carry me off the field on their shoulders.

I soon learn that our four seasons in Florida are not the same as up north. For instance, I am astonished when I learn that in the northern states the leaves fall off the trees in the fall and winter. Our seasons are hurricane season, love bug season, tourist season and fire season.

When a hurricane approaches we have about a day's notice to button up our houses. We gather round the radio, staring at its wooden veneer for the latest information. My Dad works up until the last minute that is humanly possible before the hurricane strikes. He fills those precious minutes taking down the awnings of his customers, which he does for free. "They're my customers," he explains, when my mother asks him how much he will receive in payment. "I don't charge my customers. They've already paid for their awnings."

After the hurricane passes he goes back to each customer and re-hangs every awning, again with no charge…because they are his customers. One time a radio crew from a major station follows him around as he works right up until the last moment. I am convinced my Dad is a hero…more for the fact that he never charges his customers for this service, than the danger he faces in his race against the hurricane.

Hurricanes usually come in September, which the students don't mind since it means we have a few days out of school. When one comes through, we hunker down with the family in our wooden house with the screened-in porch that wraps around one side, right across from the courthouse, where inmates are kept on the top floors. We eat Spam and Vienna sausage sandwiches and lose our power for days. Afterwards, my Dad drives us to the beach to see all the fish and sand that has blown over A1A; we sometimes find valuables, like big shells or small boats.

I have some interesting friends in high school: Barbara Anheiser of the beer family, who gives great parties. My boyfriend Gordon's best friend is Fred Wakeman, Jr. His father has just written a book called, *The Hucksters*. Fred tells us that Hollywood is going to make a movie of his Dad's book and they want Clark Gable to play the lead.

"Mr. Gable," says Fred, "thinks the book is filthy and not entertainable and is refusing the part." One day a group of us are at Fred's house playing Ping-Pong and in walks Mr. Clark Gable with Fred's Dad, in full Technicolor, his famous moustache in place. We are in shock; mouths fall open as this screen presence walks among us, smiling gently with his famous, recognizable grin. Shortly afterwards, Fred tells us that his Dad has explained his main character in the book and reels Gable in to accept the role.

I return home and tell my mother I met Mr. Clark Gable. As so many women in the south and in the 50's, my mother thinks that the movie, *Gone with the Wind* is second only to the Bible in importance and devotion. Our parents take us to see it every time it plays at the Lyric Theater, and my mother always cries at the same place, when the daughter dies from a fall from her pony.

My mother, of course, insists that I tell her every mannerism, every word that I heard coming from the lips of Mr. Gable. I revel in her undivided attention as my little brother, Hersch, and sister gather round waiting for my answers, which I, of course, embellish as much as I can by acting as though I had officially met him.

"Oh my, he is sooo handsome, not as tall as he appears in *Gone with the Wind*...but oh sooo charming, sooo nice, soft spoken...he looks each one of us in the eyes when Mr. Wakeman introduces us." (He never introduced us at all.)

Every spring, college kids descend upon Ft. Lauderdale, performing their usual pranks such as putting a shark into the hotel swimming pool. Spring also brings dances, and graduation.

My senior year I attend the prom with skinny, redheaded Gordon McCully, the best tennis player on our high school team. After the dance we drive west out to a local dive. Years later Hollywood makes a movie about our antics and calls it, *Porky's*.

For our senior class trip, and for those who can afford it, we fly an hour away to beautiful Havana, Cuba. We tour the perfume factories and visit Moro Castle. Havana is beautiful, but I quickly learn that two years of high school Spanish does not help me understand the locals at all.

On our last night in Havana a riot erupts in the bar across from our hotel. Gunfire breaks out and the police are called. "Some upstart called Fidel Castro is named as the cause of the trouble," says our Spanish teacher and chaperone, Mrs. Jett, after reading the morning paper. Fortunately, we depart after breakfast.

When it comes time to consider college I have two choices: the University of Florida in Gainesville, which has previously been an all boys' school, with a ratio of 12 guys to every gal; or, Florida State University in Tallahassee, which has previously been an all-girls' school with a ratio of 15 gals to every guy. There is no question—I talk my parents into sending me to Gatorland. I go to college, majoring in Journalism at the University of Florida, and became a Gator for life. One of the first rules I learn is that all female students must wear raincoats when wearing shorts and walking across the campus. Heaven forbid that our legs might show.

However, my college years are cut short because my parents simply can't afford to pay for my completion. By the time I finish all the college I can get, my parents move up state to central Florida, to Eau Gallie, a suburb of Melbourne, Florida.

During the summer, I apply for my first job as a secretary with Radiation, Inc., which later becomes Harris Corporation. With my first paycheck I pay down on a TV for my parents. Still living at home, I wallpaper my bedroom with a beautiful pink flowery motif. My sister, Zola, heads to Texas for better job opportunities and moves in with my aunt Lila and uncle Albert; I now have a whole bedroom all to myself. We live on the second floor, above my Dad's business. I've never lived on a second floor and it seems a lot hotter during the summer months.

I never really felt like I said goodbye to my youth until I secured that first job. I like to recall the memories of my early years. They are a gentle reminder of a kinder, slower time when we filled our lives with family vacations, and the outdoors. I like to remember the grit and "can do" attitude of my parents: the triumph of my mother over the pain and difficulty of her life; the high level of pride in my Dad's work and his commitment to his customers.

Even though I don't finish college, I never look back; never entertain any regrets, or doubts for my future. I will make the most of what comes my way because my parents have showed me how to do it.

I pay down on a car, buy some professional looking clothes and become even more determined to be the best secretary I can possibly be, until I can, somehow, someway, someday, be a writer..

CHAPTER 2

. . . .

THE JOURNEY

t's 1969—July in Florida. The sun is scorching the grass and I can almost hear the sizzle and it's only 20 minutes past 7 a.m. It's hot, humid, and sweat is rolling down my face as I walk toward the back entrance to the IBM administration building in the town of Cape Canaveral, but I don't care. The weather doesn't bother me because the launch of Apollo 11 will take place in eight days. History is already in the process of being made. The excitement is building; each day brings us closer to our national goal—and to my personal goal to be present, to write about the people and the program.

I've yearned to be a part of this historic moment for almost ten years. I've worked hard to be a part of the support team that launches three men into orbit, directs them to the moon, and brings them back safely.

I'm not a missile engineer, a programmer, an analyst, test conductor, or an executive. I'm a writer and I write about the people who make it happen. Some call it marketing communications, but I consider it a much higher calling. I'm a witness—one who can relate first hand the dedication and determination, the challenges and sorrows of the many people who make up the launch support team, not the astronauts, they already get the bulk of the accolades, but the engineers, the programmers, and the administrative crew—the guys behind the scenes of the Apollo Program.

As I approach the back door, I see our facility manager, J.L. Nelson, bursting through the double doors with both hands at exactly 7:25 a.m. Once outside he positions himself to one side as employees pass him by and enter the building. He fixes his eyes on his watch as the minutes click off. I wait inside the cafeteria, peering out the windows, curious to see what will unfold next.

Nelson was appointed facility manager for IBM's Cape Kennedy Facility more than four years earlier. He takes his position seriously and he takes himself seriously. Many joke that Hollywood's central casting secured him the part. He is glib, on the short side and as handsome as any leading man. He has black hair with a startling white strip running from the front of his forehead to his crown.

He dresses as an IBM executive should dress: white shirts, winged-tipped black shoes, conservative ties and dark suits…even in this heat. At 45, he can be extremely smooth when the occasion calls for it. Many a secretary has been charmed by his soft-spoken style. Nelson has been married for more than 20 years to his second wife, but rumors persist that he is also fond of other women.

There is another side to Nelson—he is demanding and his unpredictable temper has become legendary in only a few years. There are many occasions when his yelling can be heard through the halls causing employees to wonder who the latest recipient is for his tantrums.

Silence prevails as the Florida sun peeks through scattered clouds and rests on the faces of those approaching the building, the nervous and the dumbfounded. At precisely 7:31, he pulls every employee over to the side that has not yet passed through the door. For 30 minutes he pulls employees over until more than 20 are assembled. I recognize several managers in the group, one in particular who consistently comes in late.

At 8 o'clock he begins his speech. His "late" speech as it would be later titled.

"You're all late! You're late if you didn't pass through these doors before 7:30. This is IBM and we begin at 7:30 a.m. And in case you haven't heard, we've got eight days until launch. These are crucial times. I will not tolerate slackers.

"We've got a commitment to perform to the best of our ability. IBM has achieved a reputation of excellence—and that reputation is going to continue into America's space program. Our instrument unit is the brains behind the vehicle. And you people, this team we've assembled, are the heart and soul of our program. You've been chosen to work here at this place, and at this time, because you're among the best in the business.

"Nevertheless, there have been too many people straggling in after starting time and I will not tolerate tardiness from anyone. In the future, be at your desks before 7:30."

Someone in the group tries to speak but Nelson puts up his hand. "I don't want any excuses because—there are no excuses."

"Wait a minute," yells one guy. "I was here until 1 a.m. last night and that's been the case all week long. Right now I'm getting about five hours of sleep every night and you're yelling at me for being a few minutes late?"

"We begin work at 7:30 a.m. I didn't say anything about how late you work. You do what it takes to get your job done," says Nelson as he turns, pushes open the doors and disappears back into the building.

I walk to my office through a maze of cubicles, color-coded according to departments; the highly polished linoleum floors magnify the click of my heels. I unlock my desk and check my calendar. The most important thing I have to do today is finish the first draft of the IBM Launch Countdown Procedure. It's a fixed format; with all the same sequences, beginning seven days before launch until T-0, through liftoff and up until the Instrument Unit ceases operation and is jettisoned into the ocean. I provide the new timelines as well as comments provided to me by the test conductors. I edit it and make it current. Once printed it will be 100 pages thick, give or take 10 or 20. It will be the bible for all IBM launch and executive personnel. The deadline is to have it finished and printed by noon today and in the hands of key personnel by 1:30 p.m.

I always make my deadlines. I am dependable, dedicated, driven… something that can probably be said about everyone who works here at Cape Kennedy. My job as communications specialist is one of great responsibility and attention to detail. Nowhere in the whole world is there any more attention to detail than there is here at Cape Kennedy, especially at this time.

My deadlines include a daily one-page edition of the IBM Cape Kennedy News, an employee information vehicle. On Fridays, I put out the 4-6-page edition. I write press releases on every aspect of IBM's activities. I input to *THINK Magazine* and the monthly edition of the division paper. I write speeches for management and ghost write articles for some of the executives. In addition I put together slide shows and represent IBM at the Cape Kennedy Public Relations Association. I also give tours to the visiting high-level IBMers and their guests. As I see it, my most important job is to write about the people.

Oh yes, I'm also the coordinator for Speak Up!, a comment, suggestion and complaint program that allows employees to vent. And that little incident with Nelson and the late employees garners the most Speak Up!s on any subject ever received at the Cape.

Here I am in a job that I would pay IBM for. I think it's the best job in America right now, this minute in July 1969. Every time I flash my badge to get onsite at Cape Kennedy, I ask myself the question, "How did I get here?" How does one explain the remarkable results of the last 10 years?

CHAPTER 3

EARLY SPACE PROGRAM

M y first introduction to America's space program comes through marriage. In the late 50's I marry the first guy I seriously dated—which is the norm for most women during this time.

I meet Hank Croskeys, a tall and handsome southerner from Greenville, South Carolina, at the beach. I am petting a dog and he comes up to me with the poorest pick up line I've ever heard.

"Is that your dog? I just pulled a big tick off him a few minutes ago."

"No, I'm just petting him."

He tells me about his job with General Dynamics/Convair at launch complex 36. A graduate of Georgia Tech with a degree in mechanical engineering, he is responsible for the liquid hydrogen and liquid oxygen that goes into the 402,000 pounds of thrust for the Atlas vehicle.

Here's a glamour shot of me from the 60's

WOW! A southerner with a job, not bad looking either—we are married a year later.

In a few years, after the birth of two daughters, Hank works on Project Mercury, which includes four manned orbital flights during 1962 and 1963 that put our first Americans, John Glenn, Scott Carpenter, Wally Schirra, and Gordon Cooper in orbit.

Hank's job is to help America progress in the exciting space program. My job is to drive the kids to the nearest beach and watch all the space vehicles pass overhead. "There's Daddy's missile." I really have never relished the role of a cheerleader. I'm more of a doer.

We live, talk and eat the Space Program. If there is any conversation at all, it is about his work. I envy him. I long to be a part of such fulfilling work. It's exciting to hear about but the hours are unbelievable. Sometimes Hank doesn't come home for days and when he does, he sleeps for hours, never spending time with his family (three daughters by this time). Add to this the two-hour round trip and it is a demanding pressure for our family.

At General Dynamics, he goes to work on the Gemini flights which puts two-man teams of astronauts into orbit, including: Grissom and Young; McDivitt and White; Cooper and Conrad; Borman and Lovell; Schirra and Stafford; Stafford and Cernan, Young and Collins; Conrad and Gordon and Lovell and Aldrin.

The Atlas proves to be the most reliable rocket-booster system and is still performing today. Hank works on launches for the Surveyors, Applications Technology Satellites, Orbiting Astronomical Observatory 2, and Mariners 6 and 7. These early projects provide over 88,000 valuable photos of the moon for future manned flights.

I am raising our children by myself. When Hank and I do talk, nerves are frayed, tempers shot. He might be solving the problems of our space program but nothing gets resolved at home. He lapses into spells and doesn't speak to me for weeks. I notice perfume smells on his shirts, and even later hours. I suspect he's having an affair but really don't care. Our sex life is nil, over in a few minutes. He's never taught me anything about sex. I was a novice when we married…and still place myself in that category. My satisfaction is not his priority. I came into the marriage unknowledgeable about sex. He has killed any love I had for him. Deep down I wonder if there's something wrong with me…is it me? Or him?

He is also terribly cheap. With no money of my own, not even coin-change, I have to beg for a quarter to pay for a tennis court, providing my mother will babysit for me. If I go grocery shopping and exceed the amount of the check he has given me, I have to take out objects at the counter. I am not allowed to be a co-signer on his checking account. I have no money of my own. I feel like a prisoner…one who is totally neglected.

Now that the girls are all in school I desperately want to get a job. At breakfast one Saturday I tell Hank my desire to go back to work. He explodes, "What can you do? You can't make enough money to buy your own Kotex."

That's all the motivation I need!

CHAPTER 4

· · · · · · · · · · · · · · · ·

APOLLO BEGINS

President Kennedy sets the Apollo Program in motion on Thursday, May 25, 1961, when he addresses Congress and says: "I believe that this nation should commit itself to achieving the goal, before this decade is out, of landing a man on the moon and returning him safely to earth. No single space project in this period will be more exciting, or more impressive to mankind, or more important for the long-range exploration of space; and none will be so difficult or expensive to accomplish."

Thus begins the search for the greatest technical team, outside the united team that fought World War II, that America has ever known—the team that will meet one of the most difficult challenges of all mankind. And, if achieved will be argued and questioned for years to come. After Kennedy's assassination in 1963, the push to complete this goal is now a national urgency—and no place feels that pressure more than the Kennedy Space Center. To put a man on the moon in this decade, as Kennedy put it, means it has to happen before 1970.

Some of the many IBMers who worked at Cape Kennedy during the 60's (IBM)

Contracts go out for the launch vehicle, consisting of three separate stages: The Boeing Company wins the contract for the first stage, containing five engines furnished by the Rocketdyne Division of North American Aviation. North American also garners the contract for the entire second

APOLLO BEGINS | 25

stage, also containing five engines; Douglas Aircraft builds the third stage with one 200,000-pound thrust engine with a restart capability.

IBM is selected to provide the Instrument Unit, or IU, the brains of the vehicle. It contains a computer and the electronic control systems which will steer the vehicle to the moon and correct its trajectory in flight; on top of the IU, sits the North American spacecraft.

Making up each launch team are thousands of ground-based launch systems engineers, technicians, programmers, administrative personnel, and support crews.

Every contractor begins a massive search for the most capable, most qualified members for their teams. They scour university engineering graduates, other firms, and those presently working at Cape Canaveral to fill the most unique positions that Apollo offers. Most administrative positions are filled from the local pool.

Hank joins North American, fulfilling his dream job of being on the launch team for the Apollo Program. He is responsible for the environmental control system for the spacesuits that the astronauts wear on their flights to the moon and back.

If I thought the earlier space programs were demanding, I am in for a big surprise.

Kennedy Space Center is huge. The space agency has approximately 84,000 acres bought from the State of Florida, and an additional 55,805 acres of submerged lands, most of which lie within the Mosquito Lagoon, which is separated from the ocean by a narrow beach strip on the east, and connected with the Indian River on the west by the Haulover Canal crossing Merritt Island. The total investment: $71,872,000 and approximately 140,000 acres under the management of KSC.

The fire that occurred in January 1967, during a test that claims the lives of Grissom, White and Chaffee, also marks the space center's loss of over-confidence and the calmness that had prevailed. Changes are made, inspections tightened and Apollo becomes precision tuned. A renewed sense of dedication, urgency and attention to detail takes over.

NASA gives birth to the Manned Flight Awareness program, which stresses the importance of every person's job. A new awareness brings the absolute need for the highest degree of accuracy on everyone's part. "Even a typo can result in the loss of human life," says the posters.

NASA moves quickly to ensure that a similar tragedy will not occur in the future. A new flameproof material called Beta Cloth is substituted for nylon in the space suits. Within the spacecraft itself, technicians cover exposed wires and plumbing to preclude inadvertent contact. They redesign wire bundles and harness routings. The cabin atmosphere is changed from 100 percent oxygen to 60 percent oxygen and 40 percent nitrogen.

At Launch Complex 34 itself, technicians put a fan in the White Room for ventilation. They add water hoses, fire extinguishers, and an escape slidewire. Astronauts and crew workers can slide down this wire during emergencies, reaching the ground in seconds.

Top priority is given to redesigning the hatch. The new Apollo hatch is a single-hinged door that swings outward with only one-half pounds of force. An astronaut can unlatch the door in three seconds. The hatch has a push-pull unlatching handle, a window for visibility in flight, a plunger handle inside the command module to unlatch a segment of the protective cover, a pull loop that permits a pad worker to unlatch the protective cover from the outside, and a counterbalance to hold the door open.

After the alterations and installation of new equipment and modifications of procedures, the Apollo program, with the objective of landing on the lunar surface by the end of the decade, gets approval to continue.

I am devastated at the news of losing our astronauts, as is Hank. A gloom falls over the whole country and none feel it more than those who work at the Cape.

"Now, there is a deadline," says Hank. "Get Apollo to the moon before the ten-year period is over that Kennedy set. There's going to be the biggest push to get this accomplished on time, before the decade is out. Priorities will be established; dates will be projected. There's going to be a lot of overtime—mark my words."

And he is right. It is a demanding time. Many of the Cape employees work 16- and 18-hour shifts a day. The Cape area earns the title of number one in divorces for the whole country. Hank and I became part of that statistic. I finally file for divorce, with him promising not to "pay me one cent."

I don't want his precious money—I want my freedom. The divorce is final in six months. I come away with $100 a month for each child and the guarantee that he pays for their college education.

I want to work at the Cape more than ever now. I feel confident that I can earn my own living. But how am I going to secure a job there? I know that if I can't find a decent job to pay my way, I might lose my children. Hank remarries one month after our divorce. His wife, also previously married, brings no children into the picture. She had one child who died in infancy. I feel they are just waiting for me to fail.

I take a position with Kelly Girls, a temp secretarial firm serving the NASA contractors on the space program. I ace their typing and accuracy tests and accept my first job at the parachute building, on the Cape Canaveral side, where they fold the giant parachutes that support the descending spacecraft into the ocean.

My second assignment is with IBM as a typist for the technical writing group in their temporary Cocoa Beach office. After working several months typing manuals, IBM pays off my contract with Kelly Girls and I accept a full-time job as a production typist. I am now fully vested with IBM and the Apollo Program.

My job as typist in the publications area is grueling. I type all day long, pausing only for lunch and proof reading. The manuals are highly technical, with words I've never heard before, and rampant with so many abbreviations. After six months, I am transferred to the public relations group as secretary for six writers who write and publish press releases, manuals, speeches, slide shows, and numerous in-house brochures and pamphlets. We also have a daily paper entitled, *Cape Kennedy Today*, and we contribute to the monthly version for the entire division, as well as IBM's *Think Magazine*. In addition, the writers act as ghostwriters for the engineers and technical managers who are periodically required to publish papers in engineering magazines and trade publications.

The divorce is definitely what I want, but it proves to be a challenge to run everything by myself. The most difficult task is to secure a checking account in my own name. Hank held the checking account when we were married and the bank is reluctant to issue me one in my own name, but finally does as I beg and plead, and it is feels like a major achievement. Money is scarce. I make enough to get by—barely. I get a neighborhood boy to mow the yard and I cut the shrubs. I hire a black lady to babysit the girls every afternoon from 3 o'clock until I get home, usually around 6 p.m. Sometimes she will even start dinner. We don't spend a lot of money on extras and the girls sometimes ask, "When are we going to have meat again?"

My three daughters spend their weekends with their Dad, giving me the opportunity to catch up on housework and laundry— and to play tennis.

In the summers, the girls head to an eight-week summer camp near Hendersonville, North Carolina, paid for by Hank's parents, who live an hour away in Greenville, South Carolina. They visit the camp every Sunday. During the week I faithfully call them on IBM's Watts line to catch up on their activities.

CHAPTER 5

MY LIFE AS A SECRETARY

As secretary to Warren Collins, manager of internal communications, I am responsible for supporting him with typing and shorthand (thanks to an update class taken on Gregg's shorthand in the last year). The department is made up of three technical writers who assist with proposals and technical papers, and three internal writers who handle the PR side of the department. I support the production of all the PR writers: Ellie Bradley, Joanne Lauterbach and Tom Miller; the technical writers use a typist.

Every Monday morning there is a department meeting to go over the activities at the Cape and IBM's involvement. Warren hands out the writing assignments for the week and I take notes and keep close tabs on the many tasks. I am expected to get coffee orders from everyone and bring them to the meeting, and if Warren wants a pastry, I bring that, too.

An IBM training class held in Titusville

The most difficult thing about the meetings is the smoke. I am the only member of the department who does not smoke. Cooped up in a small office with no windows with six people smoking is the most horrendous thing I have to endure in my job. I can hardly breathe and begin wheezing as soon as I enter the room. There is no consideration for non-smokers, and nowhere to hide—almost everyone I know at IBM smokes and drinks copious amounts of coffee all during the day. I'm not a coffee drinker either; I usually have hot tea and imbibe a Pepsi at lunch.

Warren is a chain smoker. There is never a moment when a cigarette isn't connected to his body—when he walks, when he talks, when he sits—it is always there, dangling from his lips, or through his fingers.

He is also a nitpicker. I guess everyone has a boss sometime in their life that gives them grief. I can't get past the fact that he is overbearing, too controlling. He is "Big Brother" personified. I've had to learn to take up for myself, and on more than one occasion, I question his harassment as not being within the parameters of IBM's creed of 'Respect for the Individual.' Nothing gets his attention faster. Nothing gets him to back off better.

"Ellie, you interview IBM's Manned Flight Awareness nominee. Let's get that story out to the news by this weekend," instructs Warren.

"He's out at the Cape, isn't he?" asks Ellie, meaning the Kennedy Space Center, not the town of Cape Canaveral where our offices reside. I sit in the back row, as far away from the smoke as possible, taking my notes.

"Yes, line up a NASA photographer before you get out there," Warren answers. Ellie is new to the launch business, having previously worked for the Washington Post. She's a top-notch writer used to deadlines and she quickly becomes my mentor. Division headquarters hired her to ensure we have at least one seasoned writer. She's a recent divorcee who thinks the move to the Cape offers a change of venue and exciting opportunities.

I devour everything I can learn about her writing, the style, the grammar, and the proofreading tricks. Ellie's writing is crisp and to the point, yet it pulls you in and makes you want to read more. I study her press releases and articles, looking carefully at the red editing marks she inserts on the other writers' articles as I type them. She is the go-to editor for all the press releases; she checks everything and gives her blessing to anything that leaves our office.

Of course, Warren also looks over every piece of writing that is produced by the department and okays it or demands a rewrite. He formerly worked in a prison before he joined IBM in Gaithersburg, Maryland, and before that, he was in the Army. He is also a workaholic, staying every evening until 7, 8, or 9 p.m. It is a mystery to the rest of the department exactly what he is doing when he stays so late. Many think it is just for appearances. It looks good, as many of the top managers are always in their offices until dark. He probably assumes it gives him permission to come in late every day too.

"Tom, you check with the test conductor and see if there's a new slant there for a story," says Warren.

Tom is a Vietnam veteran, formerly in the Army in the public affairs office. He is short, about 5'4" at the most. He is witty, charismatic, single and a real charmer—with a love of drink and partying.

We have ten men from the IBM Cape Kennedy Facility who depart on military leaves of absence for Vietnam, two have returned so far and one gives his life for our country. Army PFC Robert E. Mackey doesn't return. The former Saturn Documentation Center clerk dies of wounds received during fighting with the Viet Cong—the first from the Federal Systems Division who dies in action in the Asian Conflict.

"Joanne, you cover the Manned Flight Awareness reception," says Warren.

"Okay," says Joanne, obviously thrilled with her duty.

One of the most sought after assignments for the writers is to cover NASA's Manned Flight Awareness reception the night before a launch. Outstanding employees from all the contractors are nominated for efforts beyond the call of duty. They are then recognized at the reception, which is attended by top executives from NASA, and the contractors, spouses and the astronauts that are assigned to the next launch flight crew.

As the meeting ends I head back to my office that I share with one other secretary, also a smoker. I learn a lot from the writers as I type their copy every day. To forward our stories on to division or corporate I use a machine called the Magnetic Tape/Selectrix Typewriter, or MT/ST. Only a few typists here at the facility have the know-how to use the machine and I am one of three who has been thoroughly checked out on it. I feel sure that this capability is one of the main reasons I am promoted to my secretarial position.

One day, being heavily burdened with typing from all the writers, with major articles, updates and procedural manuals to get out, I decide that I will just eat my lunch at my desk to make all the deadlines. I might even have to stay late to finish everything on my desk.

Warren suddenly appears in my office. I look up to the golden embers of the cigarette as he speaks, "I need you to call these 30 people on my list and invite them to a political rally at my house," he says.

"You're kidding, right?" I say as I straighten up in my chair and stop typing. No one works longer hours or produces more work than I do. I am fast and accurate and I pride myself in making deadlines. "You see all this typing, I need to get it out—it all has to go out today. Do you want me to put aside the company's business to do yours?

"Yes, I do," comes his directive.

"That's just not right, Warren. We work on government property. I can't give a higher importance to your personal work over our due dates. Those calls would take me at least an hour. I don't have an hour to spare."

"Are you refusing to do what I'm asking you to do?"

"Warren...your work is political...it has no place on government property," I say as my voice cracks. I clear my throat.

"You'll do what I ask you to do," he says, voice getting louder. "This is insubordination."

"I'm sorry, I just don't have the time."

"Well, we'll see about that," he says as he abruptly turns and leaves my office. In a few moments my phone rings. It's Leon Bill's secretary, Mary Ann, "Leon would like to see you now in his office." Leon is the manager of the entire communications department.

Great, I think, another interruption. I guess I'm going to have to call all of his 30 friends. I get to his office as quickly as I can; Warren is already seated, puffing away on his cigarette, a devious smile on his face that seems to say, 'Gottcha.'

I sit down amidst the smoke and expect the worst.

"Warren tells me you've just refused to do something he's asked you to do for him. Is that true?"

"Yes sir, it is true. I've got articles and manuals to type that have to go out today. I am really swamped. He wants me to make personal phone calls to 30 of his friends to invite them to his house for a political rally." I pause and clear my throat again. "To do that would take away at least one hour from my work. I just don't believe political endeavors take precedence over the important work I need to get done for our department," I say with conviction.

"Oh, I see, political matters." He pauses and then says distinctly. "You're absolutely right. Warren," he says, turning and looking right at him, "we cannot perform any political work on government premises. You are wrong to ask her to stop the important work that must be done, to get your personal, political work accomplished. I suggest you make your own calls from your home tonight."

"Thank you for coming in, Martha," he says as I rise to exit his office. I try not to look elated…but inside I feel a sense of relief that there is an avenue to get justice. I presented my case; Leon heard it and gave me his blessing.

I might have won that one, but Warren will not forget today. I have a feeling he will try to make my life miserable for years to come.

CHAPTER 6

• • • • • • • • • • • • • • • •

I AM PROMOTED TO WRITER

As the Cape matures with more Apollo launches the ground crew swells to over 5,000 people, all playing a part in this big puzzle called Apollo—and there are no insignificant roles in that number.

The night before the launch of Apollo 8, the crew of Frank Borman, James Lovell, Jr. and William Anders receive a surprise visit from Charles Lindbergh and his wife, Anne Morrow Lindbergh.

Apollo 8 provides a beautiful liftoff on Sunday, December 21. The crew makes a memorable telecast from lunar orbit that Christmas Eve. Anders describes the view:

"I hope that all of you back on Earth can see what we mean when we say that this is a very foreboding horizon, a rather dark and unappetizing looking place. We are now going over—approaching—one of our future landing sites selected in this smooth region called the Sea of

IBMers work inside the IU (IBM)

Tranquility. Smooth in order to make it easy for the initial landing attempts; in order to preclude having to dodge mountains. Now you can see the long shadows of the lunar sunrise. We are now approaching lunar sunrise, and for all the people back on Earth, the crew of Apollo 8 has a message that we would like to send to you."

Anders then begins to read from the Book of Genesis in the Bible, "In the beginning God created the Heaven and the Earth…." Lovell and Borman also read part of the passage and Borman concludes: "And from the crew of Apollo 8 we close with good night, good luck, a Merry Christmas, and God bless all of you—all of you on the good Earth."

The offices at our Cape Kennedy Facility are running smoothly. We are launching Saturn vehicles every three months. I quickly pick up Ellie's writing and editing style and am even at the point where I can efficiently correct grammar and mistakes while I am typing articles.

When it comes time for my annual review, I let Warren know that I want to be a writer. My goal has always been to work as a writer. The year is a good one for women. Thanks to efforts by the women's liberation movement, strides are being made all over the country to get more women involved in business positions outside of traditional secretarial categories. IBM, in turn, is now urging management to recognize this untapped resource and to promote women from within to more salaried positions. There will be no more new hires coming in at the Cape, so any positions have to be filled by current employees. With more launches and more assignments, the writers are extended as far as they can go.

My phone rings and it's Warren, asking me to come see him. I hurry in, steno pad and pencil in my hand.

"Tom's just called in sick—well, he's not really sick, he's hungover from too much drinking last night," he says. "He's got an important interview this morning and everyone else is tied up. Do you want to cover the interview and write the story?"

I squeal, "Absolutely! There's nothing on my desk that can't wait." Warren, I'm sure, got this order from above the chain of command. But, still, I am grateful to him for recognizing the possibility that I can do it.

I go to the interview, take my notes in shorthand and return to write the story. I pull the last page and the carbon sheet out of my typewriter and lay it on the top of the face-down sheets, tapping them gently to get every sheet even. I have written my first article, and shortly thereafter at 32 years of age, I am promoted to a salaried position as a writer.

Over the next year I put out a lot of copy—press releases, stories, updates, the status of our operation—it is so fulfilling, so satisfying. The days are filled with new assignments, new challenges. I am amazed that I can write technical stories so well. I now understand the machinations of the program...and if I don't grasp the technicality of what the engineers or analysts are telling me during my interviews, I stay with it, asking for more explanations until I do and can write the story so anyone can understand it. Because of the importance of our stories and the constant effort to have them correct, all articles are pushed through several layers of management for approval before they are sent out to the media, or even printed in our own IBM publications.

I can hardly wait to get to work every day. I don't even mind the hour-long drive north along A1A. I usually wake up early at 5 a.m. I shower the night before knowing that I will be rushed to get to work. I eat no breakfast, brush my teeth, dress, attach my fall, already set in tight curls, to my head, and apply my foundation and rouge.

My oldest daughter, Curran, now 12, has the task of getting her two younger sisters, Cathy, 9 and Cindy, 6, up, fed and dressed. They ride their bikes the three blocks to school.

At 5:45 I leave my house in Indialantic and drive north on A1A to work, watching the sun come up over the Atlantic Ocean on my right. I turn on the radio to catch the morning's news: "...*Allied forces drove off a communist attack after five hours of intense fighting 38 miles from Saigon.*"

Earl Nightingale's program follows the news and the rest of my morning drive is filled with music. *Can't Buy Me Love*, by the Beatles gets me awake…then the Beach Boys with *Good Vibrations*…Elvis with *Suspicious Minds*. I sing along with every song.

I arrive at the building at 6:45 a.m. As I walk through the corridors, the freshly waxed linoleum floors gleam. IBMers rush to their offices now, some with Styrofoam cups in their hands, others carrying books, reports or attaché cases. The men who are not managers, who are not required to wear suits, all have plastic pocket protectors filled with pens and sometimes slide rulers.

I greet everyone in the halls as I make my way to the bathroom, recognizing Jo Barry, my best friend at work and also our Facility Manager's secretary.

"Don't we have a rehearsal this afternoon?"

"We sure do," I respond, "as soon as you can get to the cafeteria. We'll begin rehearsing with the piano player today."

"I'll be there. We've only got a week before the facility dinner," she adds. The facility dinner is a big occasion. It is a motivational and appreciation event for all employees. Our chorus will sing several songs, with solos thrown in—and I have even written a skit. Spouses are invited, corporate and division executives will make speeches and thank everyone for our hard work. The dinner is first class. Everyone who doesn't have to stay onsite for special tests will attend.

As Jo moves beside me to share the mirror, the difference between us is magnified. I am tall, 5'9". Jo is short, 5'2". I'm a brunette with the big hair of the day accentuated with the curly fall sitting on top; Jo has short, highlighted blond hair. She is the best singer in our IBM singing group—the Missiletown Pipers.

Everyone likes Jo. She is friendly, helpful, an excellent secretary and long-time IBMer, 18 years with the company. No one is considered "long time" until they've been with the company for at least 10 years. Jo is with IBM for the long run. She was hired right out of high school in Endicott, New York, and transfers to the Cape with her husband, Dale. It is Dale who is in demand as an electrical engineer and Jo has come along in the package deal.

When IBM receives the initial contract from NASA to provide the instrument unit for the Saturn launch vehicle, management first looks within the company to find the best-qualified engineers, systems analysts, programmers and management team they can assemble. Then they conduct an outside search for specialists and support people, bringing the ranks of IBMers at the Cape to over 1200.

The complete Apollo team, including the Cape, Huntsville, Gaithersburg and Goddard, and other contractors, as well as NASA locations, directly involves slightly over 400,000 people and about 20,000 industrial and university contractors. Included are some of the country's foremost scientists and engineers. This mobilization of personnel and resources is unprecedented in history since World War II.

I apply my red lip liner, then the coral lipstick with a lipstick brush. Pale blue eye shadow is smoothed over my eyelids, then black liquid eyeliner that I draw out past my eye. A white pearl highlight goes under my eyebrows and the black mascara goes on last. I brush my bangs and check my fall to make sure every curl is in place. I step back from the mirror and find no slips or straps showing. I am "Go" for work.

As soon as I sit down my eyes spot the big piece of paper in Warren's handwriting, "Come see me.... and bring me some coffee." I stash my purse away in the filing cabinet and unlock my desk.

I stick my head in Warren's office and find him writing, with his omnipresent cigarette hanging from his lips.

"You want to see me?" I ask.

"Yeah," he answers. "Where's my coffee?"

"Warren, I don't do cookies or coffee anymore, you know that. It's not in my job description." There are several things I hold to with my new position. I stop baking cookies or cakes for birthdays—and I stop fetching coffee. If I am in a professional position I intend to act like a professional.

I now dress the part of a professional with more suits and tailored clothes. One secretary is sent home from work when she wears a pants suit to work. Following that incident a memo is sent out stating that Pants Suits are not proper attire for women and anyone wearing them will be sent home. I read *Ms Magazine* and *New Woman Magazine*. I even buy Betty Friedan's book, *The Feminine Mystique*. Damn, I am not only a professional—I'm a feminist. I believe in equal pay for equal jobs, and after knowing what my mother went through, I believe in the right to choose. I also believe in the Equal Rights Amendment.

There are a couple of negatives for a woman who wants to work and have a family, too, or "have it all", as the media calls it.

Cathy speaks up at dinner one night and says, "Margaret Ann's mother won't let her come to our house to play with me anymore."

"Why, did you have an argument?" I ask.

"No, it's because you work. She believes there should be an adult supervising and you're not here."

"My friend, Lolly, isn't even allowed to play with me anywhere, anytime, because you work," says Curran. "No one else's mother works. Why do you have to work?"

My face freezes. I am the only working Mom on my entire street—every woman that surrounds me is a stay-at-home mother, which is the norm for the day.

"I am so sorry, but I have to work now that Daddy and I are divorced. And you know what? I really love to work, too. It's important work and I'm good at what I do. IBM is good to us, too. Don't worry about those friends, you have lots of other kids who are friends who will play with you anytime."

Warren interrupts my thought process. "I need you to go see Nelson. He'd like you to take a cut at writing his welcome speech for the facility dinner. He purposely requested you. Call his office for an appointment."

Warren's demands on me have mellowed somewhat since proving myself as a writer. I am given a little more respect and it feels good—I know he is disappointed that he has to get his own coffee, but I am firm on that subject.

I call and request an appointment and Jo tells me he can see me now. I hurry over and Jo motions me to go in.

"I need some words put together for my welcome speech," says Nelson. "Thanks for a job well done…and some motivational words, too…but don't use too many 25 cent words, keep it short and to the point."

"Fine, I'll get right on it. I'll have a draft later today."

I turn and leave the office elated with the confidence he has in me to write these important words for our employees.

My first draft of his speech is accepted:

Welcome to our facility dinner. I'd like to recognize Jim Bitonti, our division president.

The countdown to liftoff of our nation's long-anticipated Apollo Lunar landing mission is entering its final years. For every one of us here at IBM Cape Kennedy, these last days and hours before launch will be etched in memory for years to come—most likely for our lifetime.

We are, at this time and place, taking part in the making of magnificent history. All that we have done, and all that we do in the days remaining, will help make Apollo's journey to another planet possible.

Because of the special significance of this mission to us—as Americans, as IBMers and as members of the NASA/industry Apollo team—you are to be congratulated for your commitment, perseverance, and dedication.

I know we've asked a lot of you—long hours, trying circumstances, difficult challenges. Nowhere is that more evident than your lost time with your family. So I'd also like to recognize the spouses tonight for enduring these heavy responsibilities and keeping the home fires burning.

The IBM Cape Kennedy team has put its finest effort into this mission, and I am confident Apollo will fulfill our highest hopes and expectations.

Now, let's sit back and enjoy this wonderful dinner and the camaraderie of our friends and spouses.

Following that little speech, I become his key person for all his future speeches and important correspondence.

My admiration for Ellie Bradley grows every day. I watch how she handles herself, how she dresses, but most of all, her writing. I envy her background in a field of true journalism. Working at the *Washington Post* had to be a great challenge. The stories she could tell, but never does; and I don't pry either.

Ellie is average height, slim, short hair, glasses, and good legs. Divorced, no children. A jovial soul, until she gets serious over a subject. She can hold her own against Warren and even Nelson, if she thinks she's right. That's the part I admire most—her strength, confidence, her self-assurance, backed up by experience.

I have never lived in a large town, let alone a huge city like Washington, D.C. Ellie worked at the *Post* for more than ten years. The only time I hear her talk about that time is when she reveals to me that her pay was much lower than the male writers. I was a secretary at the time she shared this with me and I was able to do a search of comparative salaries of the men and women writers in our department. I found that it was true here, too. The male writers receive more money than any of the female writers.

When I receive my promotion from secretary to writer my salary only jumps a little. I am classified as "salaried," which means I am not paid for overtime. I am paid a lump sum. I am still the lowest paid person in the department. I made more money as a secretary with my overtime checks. As the months and years go by I question this several times— first in my own head. Why are Tom or any of the male technical writers paid more than Joanne, Ellie and I am? I'm never late, never miss deadlines, never have hangovers, and now exclusively write all of Nelson's speeches while writing all the same kinds of things that the men do? I feel sure that my production rate is higher, too.

During one those times when I can't contain myself anymore, I am in Warren's office for my annual review and ask the question.

"Why are women paid less than the men?"

"Men have families to support."

"I have a family," I shoot back.

"Well, doesn't your ex-husband pay you something every month?"

"A little something," I add. "But all the women in our department are paid less than the men."

"All of them are single women, too."

"So you're saying that even if we do all the same work as the men, and maybe even more…and maybe even better, we'll still get paid less?"

"That's the way it is. And don't forget, Tom is a veteran."

"But, he doesn't have a family."

"He has served his country—we need to recognize our veterans," comes his quick reply.

I'm not happy with any of his answers, but at the same time I know I will get nowhere with him. It makes me feel like marching in one of those rallies that are taking place all over the country for equal pay for equal work. I reason to myself that IBM is always at the forefront of these issues. They will correct it as evidenced by my promotion out of a clerical position. It will take patience on my part and on the part of all my sisters across the United States, but change is coming.

Ellie asks me to meet her for dinner Saturday evening. Since the girls will be with their Dad and his wife, I agree. We meet at 6 p.m. at Ramon's in Cocoa Beach. As usual, she is prompt. I know I'll have to endure the chain-smoked cigarettes, but I don't want to miss an opportunity to learn from this woman.

We sit down at our table and study the menus.

"What's good here," asked Ellie?

"I love their Caesar salad and their prime ribs," I suggest.

"Fine, that's what I'll have, too."

We order no wine, only water. I don't drink alcohol at all and I've heard from others in the department that Ellie is "on the wagon," from too much hard drinking in D.C.

"So, tell me about yourself. How long have you been divorced now?" she begins.

"Almost two years."

"Have you done any dating?"

"Some…I've dated some guys I met on the tennis court. Not anyone within IBM, that's for sure. What about you, are you dating?"

"Yes," comes her surprising answer. "I've met an IBM engineer, Jim Mueller, who works at the VAB in engineering."

"That's wonderful Ellie. So quick, too."

"I'm a very private woman so let's just keep this between ourselves."

"Of course, I wouldn't repeat anything you tell me."

"Are you on the pill?" She asks.

"The pill?"

"You know, the birth control pill."

"Well, I'm not in a serious relationship yet so I see no need to take a pill."

"How many children do you have?"

"I have three daughters."

"Well, you don't want to wait until you've found someone. You never know when the occasion will present itself. You should be on it at least a month before it's effective," she says. "Tell me, did you plan your other pregnancies?"

"Plan them? No…I just had them."

"Now, you can plan how many children you want by controlling your body with the pill. It allows us to limit the size of our families. It gives women more freedom. We don't have to be faced with unwanted pregnancies. As a single woman you can have sexual freedom, more choices in your personal life."

"I've read *The Feminine Mystique* and found it interesting. Friedan claims that a housewife wants satisfaction in jobs and family. That makes sense. I can relate to that. I am bored staying home all the time, even though I love my girls dearly. I want to create, to have satisfaction in something I create…to do something meaningful," I say.

I begin to understand that Ellie plans everything, every aspect of her life, including her body. She leaves nothing to chance. We finish our salads and continue to talk constantly. I pick her brain on every subject. I figure she is at least 12 years older than me…and so much wiser.

"Do you worry about your girls…how they'll turn out because you work?"

"Yes, of course," I respond quickly. "I get pressure from my parents and some of my friends who don't work. I've always wanted to have a career. Now that I'm not married I don't have a choice. I don't receive any alimony; I just receive a little child support. I have to work."

"Your girls will turn out fine. They'll be strong, intelligent and know the importance of having a career because they will model after you. Have you ever heard of Eudora Welty?"

"No."

"Well, she mailed in her job application to The New Yorker, offering her services as a writer to perform in a job that she would love. She offered to step in for the great James Thurber, 'in case he goes off the deep end.' We all must pursue our purpose to do what we love. It brings satisfaction to us and our children because they can see the happiness our jobs bring us."

"But there has to be a happy medium. Workaholics take it to extremes," I comment.

"Yes, Madeleine L'Engle riffed on T.S. Eliot in her meditation on creativity when she states that to find fulfilling work, we stand in our own way all too often by taking ourselves too seriously to dare 'disturb the universe' in any meaningful way," says Ellie.

The following day I call my doctor for an appointment and get a prescription for the birth control pill. Of course the pills won't be covered by IBM's benefits program, but they are only a few dollars and I can afford that. Besides, I might need them someday.

• • • • • • • • • • • • • • •

CHAPTER 7

A TIME TO SING

Following the success of Apollo 8, two major tests still need to be conducted before our astronauts can attempt the first lunar landing. The lunar module has never operated with the Apollo command and service modules on a Saturn V vehicle. Apollo 9 will subject the lunar module to strenuous testing in Earth orbit and Apollo 10 will test it in lunar orbit.

The Apollo 9 lunar module arrives at KSC in June 1968, beginning the flow of equipment and preparations for the launch scheduled for February 1969. The crew consists of Jim McDivitt, David Scott and Rusty Schweikart.

With an accelerated schedule of launch in just two months, NASA and contractor launch and support teams labor steadily with six-day work weeks, by day and night shifts.

A chat with Jimmy Stewart at the Manned Flight Awareness Reception

Some problems are unearthed in the painstaking checkout process. North American Rockwell corrects anomalies detected in the digital ranging generator of the Apollo spacecraft. Grumman fixes a water glycol leak between ascent and descent stages of the lunar module. A fuel pump is replaced. The flight readiness test, which exercises electrical systems, is terminated successfully. The flight readiness review, a full-scale, detailed accounting for all organizations involved in the mission from launch through recovery is successful.

Rocco Petrone, NASA's launch director, oversees the combined NASA and contractor teams for the countdown demonstration test. During the six-day test, the vehicle tanks holding liquid hydrogen, and the first stage RP-1, or jet fuel, are loaded and the rehearsal carries down to the final minutes. Following these critical tests, the spacecraft is pronounced ready. Once the launch window begins there are no holidays for the launch crew.

My phone rings. "Martha," says Nelson. "I'd like something fun to be included in our next facility dinner. Can we have a skit? Something we can laugh at."

"Okay, any subject?"

"You're the writer, write it. Something space related cute, short. Surprise me."

"You've got it." I answer, pondering the concept. This is not something that I can seek help from Ellie for either. It has to be original and fun. I stay up all night thinking of themes. It has to do with space and then what? I have to think of something to tie it all into. What's going on in America now? Woodstock, the end of the Vietnam war...the women's movement.

Later, at the dinner, Nelson steps to the microphone in the huge convention room in the Hilton, filled to capacity with IBMers and their spouses, and delivers the speech I wrote for him, verbatim.

Following a delicious dinner of salad, tenderloin steaks, baked potatoes, green beans and dessert, Nelson returns to the stage and says, "You didn't think we'd have a great occasion like this without some excellent entertainment, did you? Let's dim the lights and catch up with a space trip in the future...."

Diane Baker plays the lead role and I have enticed several male friends from the chorus to assume the other roles. Some of the brainy, systems analyst guys build a set that resembles their version of the inside of a future shuttle. The skit is a takeoff of the science fiction futuristic movie, *2001, A Space Odyssey.* I call it the HAL skit.

The countdown begins on time February 22 and proceeds smoothly until a few days before launch when the astronauts' physician, Dr. Charles Berry, reports that the crew has contracted a mild virus and should not fly at the designated time. As a result, the terminal countdown begins at T minus 28 hours on March 1, and concludes with liftoff on time at 11 a.m. on March 3.

Monday, in a meeting with Nelson, I sit across from him taking notes as he says, "Corporate and NASA want us to do a better job of selling the space program. The space program technology will expand into the future with tremendous benefits that the average person just doesn't understand. We're just fortunate that there was a Cold War going on with Russia when we got our funding. Now we've got to inform the public of future innovations in virtually every field of science and technology. We need to get the word out because we'll need more funding for Apollo18 and 19.

"Research this subject and let's see what you come up with," he says as he stands to signal the end of my appointment. His eyes sparkle and his grin widens as he walks me out.

I begin by calling Darlene Hunt at NASA Information who sends over some interesting facts and gives me a good start. We incorporate some of the ideas in all of Nelson's speeches and even in some of the slide shows—it proves to be a great teaching tool and justification for future funding for the space program.

After work I head to the cafeteria for chorus rehearsals for our next facility dinner. Several other singers are already in place. I see Ralph, our lead singer, and Gail, a great blues singer, both black; in fact, the first blacks that I have ever come in contact with since I grew up in segregated schools. They are highly talented. Ralph works as a programmer and Gail is a typist. Ralph's voice is smooth, more like Nat King Cole—and he can sing anything. Gail is an alto with a sexy-sounding voice. Joanne and Jo, both from my building, are also in the chorus, as well as Pete Theobald from engineering at the VAB.

Bob Ehrhardt is the top engineering manager and second in command after Nelson. Born in Jersey City, New Jersey, he is probably the sharpest technical guy at IBM's Cape Kennedy facility. He's also a veteran in the Army. He's known for his selflessness and commitment to excellence; a straight shooter whose eyes never stray in his marriage. A sincere and humble man, friendly to all, soft-spoken, who never raises his voice to his employees. All of us in the chorus feel honored that he is taking the time to be a part of our group. Not only does he have a beautiful voice, he can back it up with experience in other choruses, too.

There are 18 in our chorus, nine women and nine men, led by Leon, our director and head of the entire communications area. Leon brings a great background of music direction. He's the one who first suggests the chorus and finds hardy approval from top management. Leon has no trouble finding the right candidates for the chorus. Some are genuine singers, like Jo who sings with the Sweet Adelaide's, or Bob and Dave who have been in other choruses; others just want to be part of the group. As a result, we practice regularly and perform at every facility dinner.

As we sit waiting for Leon to arrive, Jo brings over an *IBM Song Book*, published sometime in the 20's. The list of songs about IBM includes many. We'll perform the most well known of the songs, *Ever Onward*.

Leon enters the cafeteria and his very presence instills quiet respect and admiration. "Good afternoon," he says as we all repeat his greeting together like school children. "Let's begin with *For All We Know*. Ralph, I'd like you and Gail to do the beginning as a duet, the sopranos and altos will come in with 'Let's take a lifetime to say, I knew you well'; followed by the men on the next line."

Our rehearsal lasts for a little more than one hour so I am hungry by the time I reach home at 6:45 p.m. I quickly make a spaghetti sauce, boil some pasta, and make a salad. After dinner I help with homework, see that the girls have their baths and finally sink into bed at 9:30.

On my ride to work the next morning, I am surprised to see Gail about four miles from our office, walking to work. I know she's just found out that she's pregnant again. She already has two other babies' ages one and three, that she's raising by herself. I also know she owns her own car. After I pass her, I pull over. She recognizes my car and hurries to open the door.

"Can I give you a lift, Gail? Is your car in the shop?"

"No, Lorenzo got it and won't bring it back."

"Well, how long has he had it?"

"'Bout two weeks now."

"Have you been walking to work very morning for the past two weeks?"

"Yes, I have. I call him but he don't answer."

"What? He has your car and you're walking to work every day? Where does he work?" I ask, feeling my teeth start to grind.

"He's in the Air Force at Patrick Air Force Base."

"Do you know the building?"

"Yes, I sure do."

We arrive at the IBM building and I stop the car, look straight at Gail and say, "You go in and ask your manager for an hour off. I'll tell Warren that I'm going to help you get back your car. I'll meet you in the cafeteria."

I hurry down the halls, go straight into Warren's office and begin speaking. "I need a little time off this morning. When I was driving to work I picked up Gail, walking to work…and she recently confided in me that she's six-weeks pregnant. Her boyfriend has confiscated her car for the past two weeks and left her to walk to work every morning. I'm going to Patrick Air Force Base to get her car back." I didn't ask, I told him. "Is that okay with you?"

Surprised, he answers quickly. "I understand, sure go ahead."

"Thanks, I'll be back as soon as I can."

I head to the cafeteria and wait for Gail, who shows up wearing a smile on her face, obviously delighted that someone is helping her. Once inside the car, I ask what I have been wondering all along. "Is Lorenzo the father of your baby?"

"No, that would be my last boyfriend."

"Is your last boyfriend the father of your other children?"

"No."

"Do any of these guys help out with your children's expenses?"

"No, never have."

"Gail, this is a new age. We have access to birth control pills, we can plan our future. We don't have to be in poverty because of too many children. We have control now." I realize I sound like Ellie.

"I know I shoulda been taking that birth control pill, but I just didn't get 'round to it."

We arrive at Patrick Air Force Base and pull into the parking space for visitors.

"What's Lorenzo's last name?"

"Brown."

"Let me handle this. I'm going to be your attorney."

We both walk in and approach the receptionist. "I'm representing Ms. Gail Taylor. I'd like to speak with Lorenzo Brown's commanding officer."

"Certainly," says the 30-ish woman with thick glasses. "One moment please." She disappears into one of the offices down the hall and returns with a handsome man in uniform.

"I'm Colonel Lamb, may I help you?"

"Yes," I reply. "I represent Ms. Taylor here," holding my hand on Gail's shoulder. "One of your men, Lorenzo Brown, has confiscated Ms. Taylor's car and has held it in his possession for the past two weeks.

Ms. Taylor has tried numerous times to reach him to no avail. We have come for the keys to her car."

"Certainly," he says. "I'll get Lorenzo in here. Please have a seat."

"Thank you," I say as Gail and I sit down and wait. After five minutes Colonel Lamb walks back into the waiting room with Lorenzo beside him. The colonel speaks first:

"Lorenzo, are you in possession of Ms. Taylor's car?"

"Yes, sir."

I speak immediately, "Well, we'd like the keys back to her car right now." Lorenzo reaches into his pants pocket and presents the keys to Gail.

"You also need to give her $10 for the gasoline you've used for the past two weeks." He reaches into his pants again, pulls out his wallet, selects a $10 bill, and hands it to Gail.

"Thank you," I say. "Thank you Colonel for assisting us in this matter."

"You're very welcome."

As Gail and I head toward the door, Lorenzo walks over to Gail and asks, "Who is that woman?"

"That's my lawyer," she says loudly with strong conviction.

• • • • • • • • • • • • • •

CHAPTER 8

APOLLO 10

As the president expresses the nation's admiration for Apollo 9, KSC crews transfer Apollo 10 from the VAB to Pad 39B. This will be the first launch from that site. This time the astronaut crew of Tom Stafford, John Young and Gene Cernan, will fly to the moon, separate the lunar module, dubbed Snoopy, descend to within 50,000 feet of the lunar surface and then rendezvous and dock with the command ship and return to Earth.

I head to the security office to select a government vehicle from the pool furnished by NASA for Apollo contractors. I sign the log sheet indicating my destination, purpose and estimated time of return and give it to Doris Brown, a 50-ish woman, also a local. There are six cars available, all Plymouths, but only two have air conditioning. It's almost 20 miles to the VAB from our building in Cape Canaveral and without air in the Florida heat I will be sticking to my clothes when I arrive.

"Any cars left with air conditioning?"

Rollout is always a great day. (NASA)

"One," comes her reply.

"I'll take it." Doris hands me the keys and writes down the license number next to my registration. I am smiling, so happy to get one of the cars with AC. I stop by Ellie's office and wait for her to get off the phone. She is going out to the VAB with me today. Ellie holds up her hand, signaling me with one finger, indicating she's almost through with her conversation.

"I'll be out there in about a half-hour. I'm leaving now," she says to the person on the other end. She slams the phone back in the cradle and looks at me, "Okay, let's go."

Once in the parking lot we head directly to the spaces allotted for Government vehicles and match the license plate with the one typed on the plastic key ring. Parking is always a problem at KSC but with a Government car I can park in the designated parking slots at the entrance to any building on the spaceport. I throw my purse and attaché on the back seat and wait for Ellie to settle in, and then start the car, adjusting the air conditioning and rearview mirror.

I leave the parking lot and drive north around what is referred to as "horseshoe bend."

"It was around this bend that a drunk driver struck a car filled with KSC employees who had been working late for a launch. All were killed," I say. "I always try to remember them when I take this path. The drunk driver wasn't even hurt and he hit them head-on, leaving seven kids without dads."

I stop at the security gate to Cape Canaveral Air Force Base. We each remove our badges and hold them up to the windshield so the guard can check the photos against our faces.

"I always get a thrill when I show my badge to the guards," says Ellie. "It gives me passage into these magical, historical premises. We are so fortunate to be among those who can enter these sacred grounds."

"There's always been tight security. I imagine to keep saboteurs and spies out. I remember a time when checkpoint lines were limited to only one guard; traffic would be backed up for miles. Some of the employees going through the lines thought the guards really didn't pay close attention to the badges. How could they with such quick entrees? One KSC guy decided to test the accuracy of the badge checks. He swore that he just held up his pack of Lucky Strikes and was admitted," I say.

To reach the John F. Kennedy Space Center, we first pass through Cape Kennedy's Air Force Station, located on the beach side, and then go west over the Banana River to Merritt Island where the Center is located. As I pass the Air Force side, we can see the Mercury gantry towers spread out like oil derricks along the coast. To our left are huge mounds with stored propellants buried underneath.

Seagulls are patrolling the area for breakfast as a jet leaves the skid strip directly overhead and sends them flying. After passing through the Cape Canaveral side, we turn left and head over the causeway road. The Titan silos are the first buildings to come into view—two of them against a bright, blue sky.

"The pads on the Cape side were built to handle nothing larger than an Atlas missile with its 388,000 pounds of thrust," I begin to explain. "Let me give you my spiel…the one I give to all the VIP's that I have on my tours. I've had to memorize every location around the Cape so that I can accurately tell our visitors the history and function of all the places on Kennedy Space Center.

"In 1962, Kurt Debus, then director of the Center, had his engineers design launching facilities to accommodate between five to ten million pounds of thrust. The engineers chose land on Merritt Island, slightly to the west of the old beach-front pads. This parcel became Launch Complex 39.

"Just as the Banana River separates the island from the rest of Cape Kennedy, the Indian River separates Merritt Island from the Florida mainland. Most of Merritt Island is a bird sanctuary, filled with citrus groves and wild, exotic birds and alligators. Many of the citrus trees still remain and in early spring the sweet smell of blossoms permeates the island," I say.

As we cross the Banana River the land becomes marshy with reeds shooting from shallow, green canals. A white Crane balances on one leg and a pair of Least Tern birds fly overhead. We pass the parachute building on the left where the huge Apollo parachutes used for reentry and splashdown are packaged on regular operating tables measuring 185 feet long.

"I held a temp job at the parachute building for about three weeks and found it fascinating to see a huge parachute systematically stuffed into a small box by a vacuum-like press," I add.

"This next building on the left is the simulator building where the astronauts train on the Command Module and Lunar Module mock-ups, or simulators. That big building next is the giant Headquarters building."

"I assume that's where Debus, Launch Director Rocco Petrone, and all the other NASA executives work," says Ellie.

"Yes. It is. One time I had a NASA photographer taking a photo of an IBMer in front of that pond when an alligator slid off the bank and headed our way. This is no ordinary alligator; he is as tame as an alligator can be tame. Many of the KSC employees spend their lunch hours around the pond and have him literally eating out of their hands. When I received my photos back, there is the 'gator in the background."

As I take the next right turn going north, we once again have to present our badges to access the road to the VAB.

"The VAB was originally called the vertical assembly building, but shortly thereafter was changed to vehicle assembly building," I say.

It now dominates the view in front of us. The flat Florida landscape, dotted with tall pine trees, one with an eagle's nest, is no match for the magnificence of the building that lies at the end of the road. At one mile away it appears massive, but it is a solitary structure with nothing to compare it to except a water tower on the right.

"See that water tower over there? A water tower is usually the tallest structure in town. Here, next to the VAB it looks like a miniature toy," I say. "Until Boeing built its sprawling aircraft plant in Seattle, the VAB was the largest building in volume in the world—129,482,000 cubic feet, 525 feet high, 716 feet long and 518 feet wide. More than 50,000 tons of structural steel was used in the framework, enough for 30,000 automobiles. Because of the building's size, a special air conditioning and ventilation system had to be installed to prevent the formation of clouds in the vast area."

"Wow, you really do have those figures memorized. You're a walking encyclopedia," says Ellie with a giggle.

"Now, please turn your gaze eastward," I say, imitating a tour bus driver. "To the east sits the majestic Saturn V vehicle on the pad. Complex 39, home of the Apollo/Saturn vehicles, taxed the ingenuity of the finest construction team NASA could assemble. *Architectural Forum Magazine* described the project as 'one of the most awesome complex construction jobs ever attempted by earthbound men.'

"The majority of space employees work inside the VAB shaping the Saturn V, stage-by-stage, working on moveable launch platforms on which the rockets are assembled and from which they are launched. After assembly, the Saturn V is moved atop one of the two, 45-story crawler-transporters, and tediously and slowly, at 3 mph, makes its way to the launch pad. The crawler will also carry the service structure to the pad after the mobile launcher and Apollo/Saturn V have been positioned over the flame trench where it will remain until seven hours before launch when liquid hydrogen propellant is loaded in the upper stages.

"Next to the VAB at 3.5 miles from the pad, is the Launch Control Center, or LCC, from which the preparations are monitored and controlled through major testing and launch. The LCC is four stories high, containing four levels; it monitors and tests every component that goes into an Apollo vehicle. Space workers think of it as not so much a building as almost a living brain. Computers and consoles are linked directly with the Saturn V while undergoing preparations in the VAB, and with the Apollo spacecraft in the Manned Spacecraft Operations building. From firing rooms in the LCC, the launch crews monitor and control the multiple technical operations performed in the course of checkout, mating, testing, fueling and launching. The Firing Room crews watch the rocket liftoff through huge windows in the east wall," I say as we pull into our parking space.

"Have you been across the catwalk yet?" I ask.

"No, but I've heard about it."

"Let me take you up there. You have to experience it, to understand the mentality of the VAB."

"Okay, I've got time before my meeting starts."

We head inside the VAB and take the elevator up to one of the very top floors. As we exit the elevator, I explain, "Now this is just a simple catwalk to get to the offices on the other side of the VAB. But prepare yourself. Follow me."

As we both walk onto the catwalk, a loud chorus of whistles, catcalls and various other sounds brings the workers from out of nowhere. The sound becomes almost deafening.

"Gimme those tits…. I'd like to ride that butt…I want that for dessert," came the catcalls.

"My God," says Ellie. "Are those sounds for us?"

"Yes, they are."

"How demeaning. I am embarrassed," says Ellie, as she hurries her steps to the other side.

"That's the way women are treated here at the VAB…never at our office, or any IBM office. Rather than ask the men to give women respect, the women have to change their attire in certain areas around the vehicle," I explain. "In other words, it's our fault because of the way we are dressed."

"Thanks for the tour. I'll know who to ask when I need exact info on KSC," says Ellie. "I'll see you later. I'm off to my interview. I'll get a ride back with one of the secretaries at the end of the day."

NASA's contractors are not allowed to take photos, or provide photographers. A request for photo coverage has to go through NASA where photographers are assigned to each writer and meets them onsite. I hurry down to the entrance to the LCC where I meet my photographer, Jake Struthers.

"Hi, Jake, I was hoping you'd be assigned to me today." Jake is a jolly, robust individual with a crew cut. He is my favorite of approximately 12 photographers that make up the pool. He is witty and fun. He also doesn't hurry me and goes out of his way to get a shot that might be a little bit different.

"I sure am, doll. What's our subject?"

But then, on the other hand, he does call me "doll."

"We're going to firing room 1 to interview our test conductor. I'd like to get some photos of him with his launch jacket and headset on…by his console. Things are really going to get busy around here so if I don't catch him for this interview this week the opportunity might go away."

"Fine. Let's go."

We walk in tandem toward the entrance to the LCC, a structure extending diagonally from the southeast corner of the VAB. The LCC houses four firing rooms, and is the equivalent of a blockhouse. Underneath the floors are miles of cable that spit out billions of bits of data between the center and the pad. Every critical component's temperature or pressure is monitored constantly and the results displayed in summary form on more than a hundred computer terminals in the room. If all the data coming from the Saturn V were printed, it would fill 300 pages each second.

Not everyone who works in the VAB is allowed to enter into the firing room. A specific number on my badge permits me access. My badge gives me access to any location, including the pad. To receive this special badge I am blessed with a 'top secret' clearance.

As we enter firing room 1, the massive steel shutters that protect the windows during launches are only partially open. The view through the window reveals the launch pad with the Saturn V poised in all its grandeur.

The room is filled with rows of consoles. NASA officials occupy the first row, the closest to the window. The prime contractors, their launch personnel, the test conductors, back-up test conductors, and top management fill the remainder of the room. IBM is on the third row, middle. During launch every person in the room wears a special launch jacket, or windbreaker, sporting the logo of his company in bold letters on the back.

"Why are test conductors always the good looking ones?" asks Jake, as Ed walks toward us at IBM's consoles.

"If the astronauts are the heroes to the American public, the test conductors are the quarterbacks for the prime contractors," I reply. "They're highly respected, intelligent, top achievers and dedicated. They run the team. With that kind of buzz going for them its no wonder the women around here adore them. Have you ever seen a quarterback that wasn't good looking?" I ask.

The median age for engineers at the Cape is 26. Ed Goodwin is 30; a southerner from Charlotte, North Carolina, who attended Georgia Tech, majoring in aerospace engineering and graduating in the top three percent of his class. He joined IBM right out of college, at the inception of its space endeavors. Since coming to the Cape, he has excelled from the beginning and is quickly groomed to be one of the four IBM test conductors. Each TC is assigned to a specific Apollo vehicle. As the TC for Apollo 11, Ed will be the reporting point for all activity on the IU from the time it arrives aboard an oversized transport plane, called the Super Guppy, at the Skid Strip, through liftoff.

The article I plan for Ed will be titled, "A Day in the Life of a Test Conductor." When I call him to set up an interview he suggests that I just follow him around for one whole day so I can see first hand exactly what he does with his days. My manager, Warren, is onboard and top management gives me permission to go any place that Ed's work takes him for one whole day.

We begin promptly at 8 a.m. at the IBM launch team meeting, then a NASA contractor meeting, followed by his participation in a one-hour system test. At lunch we eat together in the VAB cafeteria.

"You really enjoy your job. It shows," he says.

"You bet I do. It's one of those once in a lifetime kind of jobs. I'd pay IBM for this job. It's a great ride, just as much as those guys who fly atop the vehicle."

"You're also beautiful," he says, catching me off guard.

"Thank you."

Ed sports a boyish grin on his 5'11" slender, muscular frame. He also has a crew cut, like most every other guy at the Cape. His eyes light up every time he sees me and I feel myself elevated to a new degree of joy. I am so impressed with him. Have been for some time. Call it infatuation, a crush, chemistry, or just plain lust. He is bright, cute and his confidence shows through…but married, with no children. His wife works as a secretary for the Boeing Company, the prime contractor for the first stage of Saturn.

I have tried to fight the impulse, the attraction, but my defenses just crumble every time I see him. Since my divorce from Hank I am practically love-starved. It has been some time since a man held me in his arms, including the last two years of my marriage. I know I have the passion but whether or not my body responds is the mystery that I am trying to solve.

Ed is another question. Why is he pursuing me so strongly? He's married.

I have never been attracted to a married man before. I am smitten with no remedy in sight. I want to be loved but I am a novice—I don't know how to protect my heart. I take out my steno pad and ask my first question.

"You were here when the Apollo disaster occurred. Any thoughts on that day and where it led us?"

"I'll never forget the date: January 27, 1967. We were in full swing for the first flight of an Apollo that would carry astronauts. We had months of delays and developmental problems but we finally got a launch date: February 21. The three astronauts—Grissom, White and Chaffee—had been training for months for the earth-orbital mission. The spacecraft was in place on the Saturn 1B at Pad 34. We were in final checkouts. The crew was training the Block 1 version of the Command Module. Block 2, the more advanced version would take them to the moon. Block 1 was used for testing, but it didn't have the docking tunnel to crawl out of the vehicle. It had been designed before the lunar-orbit rendezvous method was decided upon. All the test conductors were in the "white room" in the old blockhouse.

"Hell, it wasn't even considered hazardous because the bird wasn't fueled. We were all relaxed—there were no emergency crews, no firemen, no doctors. They entered the spacecraft around 1 p.m. Grissom noticed a strange odor in his suit. But nothing was found. We experienced some static and bad connections and he barked at us to 'Get with it out there.'

"Just before 5:45 we were going to switch from external to internal power and we had a glitch that stopped the countdown. We never resumed the count. Just after 6:30 one of the crew said casually, 'Fire...I smell fire.' Then one of the others yelled, 'Fire in the cockpit!'

"The sealed hatch wouldn't open. There was no automatic release button to unscrew it—no time to reach for a ratchet. Then those words that haunt me to this day, 'We're on fire! Get us out of here!'

"It was a horrible sight, unbelievable. We were all in a state of shock. We questioned ourselves, the future of the program. Was it really worth the great risks? Even though IBM wasn't directly involved in any element of what went wrong—we all, every single person, man or woman at this facility—came away looking at ourselves, our commitment, differently. We knew the astronauts; they were our friends. It hurt like hell. I had nightmares for months afterwards."

I am moved to moist eyes but collect myself and ask the next question.

"Did you believe that we'd now be so close...that the day would actually be upon us when we will be going to the moon?"

"I think we all felt a need to prove ourselves to the world. I know guys who were literally killing themselves after the fire working 18 hours a day. The contractors who did assume responsibility acted quickly with design changes. An in-depth review of all spacecraft systems took place; they restricted the use of combustible materials, rescue procedures were improved, and a quick-opening hatch was provided.

"New fire-resistant spacesuits were designed. Mock-ups of the spacecraft underwent severe fire tests. Minute attention to every detail was stressed so that there was good that came from that day. Some of us were cruising along in our perfect world of automation with only technical glitches. We just didn't think deeply enough. We weren't very realistic about the possibility of losing lives.

"Hell, when you're looking at six million parts, the various systems, and exact performances by all sorts of people that have to be perfectly merged together to make this successful, it's mind boggling. We've spent eight years and $24 billion on Apollo and we're about to see a return on all those efforts."

"I understand that's when the Manned Flight Awareness Program was created, too," I say, as I continue with my notes.

"That's right. NASA jumped into action with a motivational program to recognize quality and attention to detail, but most importantly, to instill awareness of our most important part of the entire equation— human life. The program instills a sense of importance and pride in everyone's job. There are no insignificant jobs in this business when human life is at stake. Every job can affect the lives of the astronauts— from a secretary typing the correct set of numbers, to an engineer conducting a final test.

"We all have to be aware that there are lives at stake. There will always be an unknown when you're dealing with so many different factors coming together. But, God willing, we'll cut down the odds by each person performing to the best of his ability."

I look deep into his pale blue eyes and feel his intense sincerity. What a man, I think. What a time! Is it the excitement of all that is happening around me—or is it just my longing to be loved?

Several days later, the launch window opens for Apollo 10 on May 18th. At 12:45 p.m. NASA's Don Phillips, the test supervisor, heads up the countdown team occupying firing room 3 of the Launch Control Center.

While the astronauts intensively rehearse rendezvous and docking in the simulators, the launch team prepares for final countdown. The launch instant is exactly on schedule at 11 minutes before 1 p.m., Sunday, May 18.

Weighing nearly 6,400,000 pounds, since this is the first time Saturn V is carrying its full payload of all three modules, the vehicle moves with seeming deliberation and then accelerates rapidly as the five powerful engines of the first stage gulp propellant at a rate of 15 tons per second. IBM's instrument unit signals perfectly through roll sequence, jettison of the escape tower, first stage cutoff and second stage powered flight; cutoff of the second stage and third stage burn until it achieves orbit 11 minutes, 52.8 seconds after leaving Pad B. Two orbits are spent checking out the spacecraft and then, over Australia, the IU gives the "go" to head for the moon and translunar injection. The third stage engine is restarted, burning for 5 minutes, 42 seconds, increasing the velocity from 17,400 miles per hour to 24,250 miles per hour. IBM's IU performs flawlessly and is then ejected into the ocean.

Eight days and three minutes after leaving Pad B, Apollo 10 splashes down three miles from the Pacific aim point east of Samoa. The dress rehearsal for the lunar landing has been completed.

Following the customary debriefing period, the crew returns to the Cape on June 12 to face the 10,000 NASA and contractor employees jammed into the VAB.

Speaking to the team that put them into space, Stafford says, "There are only a few ways in the English language that we can say thank you, but from the three of us, we can never say that enough to all you people." To which John Young adds, "The difference between mediocrity and greatness is this launch test team—trouble shooting in real time, getting the vehicle ready under the very real pressure of trying to meet the window, and by golly, you made it. You're the greatest and we thank you."

Cernan concludes by saying, "This is a great team, a fantastic team. You're not on our team, we're on your team, and all I can say is that we're proud to be on it." After expressing their gratitude, they traverse the long walk through the transfer aisle, shaking hands, accepting congratulations and beaming with pleasure. It is a union of exceptional, extraordinary people.

CHAPTER 9

. . . .

I BECOME A SAFETY HAZARD

It is after work on a Friday that Ed, our test conductor, and I check into the Holiday Inn in Titusville. The room overlooks the Indian River to the east with the VAB visible in the background. As soon as he closes the door behind him, he reaches for me, takes my hands in his and kisses them. He kisses my lips, my neck. I feel my cheeks flush and my pulse race.

"I have wanted you ever since the moment I laid eyes on you strutting through the firing room with your NASA photographer chasing after you," he says.

I can't believe we're actually here, I think. I feel clumsy, not sure of my next move.

He kisses me again gently on my lips. Tenderly he leads me to the side of the bed and begins undressing me. He unzips my dress and it falls

The three IUs await orders (IBM)

to the floor and with it all inhibitions and fears. I want him too. I need him for this moment in time.

I really don't know much about sex or about my body. I was raised in a devout manner, void of any conversations about my body. There were never any classes about women's sexuality at college. No talks from my parents, not even when I got married at 19 did they take me aside and give me a few hints. Hank never taught me anything either. I question myself…have doubts about whether I can ever achieve something called bliss. I become keenly aware that there is much more to my development as a woman than reading about the feminist movement. Should I do research, just like I would in writing an article, to find the solutions?

The third stage is erected atop the first and second stages (NASA)

Jake Struthers, the photographer, jolts me back to real time and reality as we stand together in the massive firing room.

"Do you want all black and whites? Any color?"

"No color today. Just shoot black and whites. When can I get the contacts back?"

"Two days," he answers.

There are a dozen or so people in the firing room working at their consoles, most of them talking on phones. No major tests are being conducted today.

There are only a handful of women who actually work at the VAB. I know of only two female engineers, but not any women assigned to a console in the firing room. There are women inspectors, secretaries and programmers. The ratio of men to women is probably 400 to one.

I glance at the clock that is conveniently placed next to the digital countdown clock that ticks off the seconds backwards during launch. Today I am again meeting Ed to take a few more photos and let him go over the draft.

Ed's presence is felt in the room as soon as he opens the door, heading straight towards me. He's dressed in full launch attire for the photo shoot. Dark pants, white long sleeved shirt, tie, and the light blue, IBM logo on the back of his white windbreaker, headset in his hand.

"Just tell me what you want. I'm all yours for a half-hour."

"Let's begin with some shots by your console. Just make it natural—just as if you'd be participating in the countdown," I suggest. He puts his headset on and plugs it into the console. Jake begins shooting first from one side, then the other.

"Don't smile so much, this is supposed to be serious," I say.

"It's hard to be serious about this sort of thing."

"Well, it just comes with the territory for being the Apollo 11 TC."

"Don't say that too loudly. These guys will never stop kidding me."

I glance up to see several guys at consoles now looking our way and grinning. After a few more shots Jake let me know that he has plenty and adds, "By the way, a couple of astronauts are visiting today. Not the Apollo 11 crew but some of the others. They're supposed to be up there at the IU level talking to your engineers."

'Up there' is the 300-foot level of the vehicle where the IU sits atop the Saturn vehicle, where it is fitted between the third stage and the lunar module.

"That's wonderful. Let's go up and get some photos. You have time don't you, Jake?"

"I've got another 15 minutes before I have another job. If we could get up there right now I can do it."

"I've got 15 minutes. I'll go with you," offers Ed.

"Okay, let's go."

Jake stops in his tracks. "Wait a minute…you can't go up there dressed like that. You know if you're wearing a miniskirt, you'll be a safety violation."

That stupid, anti-women rule makes my blood curdle, yet there it is published in NASA's Safety Book. *A woman is not allowed to visit on any levels around the platform of the vehicle, above the ground floor if she is wearing a dress or a miniskirt. Such an infraction will result in a safety violation for the entire company. Women must be attired in either pants or coveralls at all times.*

"Well, I don't have time to run over to Safety and get some overalls, put them on and get back before the astronauts leave. I'll just take my chances. What could they do to me anyway? Let's get our hardhats."

"They'll give you a Safety Violation," says Jake.

"Let's go," I say as I dash toward the door.

A woman's presence in the VAB is a rare sight, especially one in a miniskirt. My presence evokes catcalls, whistles and quite a bit of attention. The fear, as NASA sees it, is that the men could become so entranced with watching a woman in a miniskirt that they might accidentally lose orientation and fall from one of the platform open areas. What gives credence to this is the way the men act...not the way the women are dressed. Of course, they must have reasoned that there is no stopping this kind of behavior from the men, so the women must change their attire. I feel like writing to Gloria Steinem to tell her about this rule.

"Just look around you. You see how you're disrupting the men already and you're still on the ground floor," says Ed as the whistles and catcalls begin.

We board the over-sized, glass-sided elevator and Jake pushes the button for the top level. The stacked Saturn V vehicle is directly to our right, no more than ten feet away, as we pass stage by stage.

"This first stage booster is the biggest aluminum can ever built," says Ed. "Its valves are as big as barrels, its fuel pumps bigger than your refrigerator, its pipes big enough for me to crawl through, and its engines, the size of your car. And that's just the first stage. With the spacecraft on top of these three stages the entire baby stands 363 feet tall…six stories higher than the Statue of Liberty.

"This mobile launcher has steel arms to hold the rocket in place through all the tests and up to seconds after ignition. Look up and around the vehicle. You'll see that all the work stations are cut out to accommodate the vehicle."

"Yes, they're all shaped in a half-moon," I notice.

"This enables the work crews to work around the various stages."

The elevator brings us to an abrupt stop at the IU level. Ed takes my hand and leads me to the edge of the platform.

"Now, look down and then look up. There are no guardrails, only a small chain link hangs across the area. It's a complete drop off."

I glance up and down and see about a dozen workers casually walking back and forth with nothing to protect them from falling or tripping.

"Can you imagine a workman down below looking up to you on this level, trying to get a little peek under your miniskirt? How great do you think his concentration would be? What if he dropped a wrench? It might kill someone. He might even lose his balance and fall. These men are important to Apollo. So with all our ingenuity, all our foresight, we have not come up with a solution to the dangers of miniskirts."

"Okay, let's get our pictures and get out of here," I say as I try to absorb the idea that my miniskirt could be a source of death.

Jake goes over and asks one of the inspectors if the astronauts have come through yet.

"No, they haven't."

"Which crew are they?" I ask.

"I hear it's the crew who'll fly Apollo 14: Shepard, Roosa and Mitchell."

It is customary for the flight crews who are not immersed in training for immediate missions to make goodwill visits. They want to be seen by the ground crews, to establish rapport, to get to know the people in whose hands they place their lives.

Moments later, the elevator door opens to three smiling astronauts, dressed in orange jumpsuits. The IBM engineers, already informed that the astronauts are to talk with them, have their hands extended, welcoming them to their level.

Jake has already started clicking his camera, moving from one side of the group to the other. I take the initiative and move right in front of Alan Shepard and extend my hand.

"Good morning, Commander. I'm with IBM and I'd love it if you'd pose for a photo with our Apollo 11 test conductor."

"I think that can be arranged. That's what we're here for. Where would you like us?"

"How 'bout right in front of our IU?"

"We sure depend on the IU. How are your tests running so far?" he asks Ed.

"Everything's on schedule and looking good."

"Let's see, the IU weighs 4750 pounds and contains the electronics and electrical equipment, including a computer, for the guidance and navigation for our flight. It's what ignites and shuts down the engines and monitors their performance," states the slim, 5'8" former Navy commander and first American in Space. His smile exudes friendship and warmth.

"Looks like you've done your homework," I say.

Shepard smiles, "And believe me, there's a lot of homework to do in this job." He glances around at all the IBMers assembled and says to them, "Keep up the good work. We're all counting on you." He motions a farewell sign to me and disappears in the crowd with Roosa and Mitchell, heading for another office and another contractor.

My smile spreads across my face. I revel in the spontaneity of the event. It happened so fast and we have just made it in time. It couldn't have been better if we had planned it. Jake looks over at me and shakes his head, each of us grinning at each other. I can hardly wait to get those contacts back. What a coup!

Just as we head for the elevator, a security guard approaches me, clipboard in hand.

"I'd like to see your badge, please," he states firmly.

I put on my sweetest charm, unclip my badge and hand it to the guard. Opting to play dumb, I ask, "Is something wrong with my badge? I do have clearance to come up here."

"You can't come up here without pants," he says.

"I have pants on," I reply as Ed and Jake giggle.

"Not underwear pants. You have to wear long pants, or a jumpsuit. The legs have to be covered. I'm going to issue you a security violation and you'll have to surrender your badge."

Gone is my charm. "Surrender my badge? I need my badge to get out here for my interviews. How do you think I can do my job? Can't you just give me a warning? This is my first ticket. I've never gotten a violation before. I'll never do it again, I promise."

I am now begging—no, groveling. "Look, this man is our test conductor. He'll tell you we just wanted to get some great photos of our people with the astronauts. Nothing devious. Right in, right out."

"That's correct, sir. It was just a spur of the minute thing. We were only here for a few seconds," adds Ed.

"What's your name? Let me see your badge." Ed hands him his badge. The guard writes down his name and badge number and hands it back to him.

"You're getting a violation too. You should have known better than to bring her up here. But I am returning your badge, sir."

Oh great, I think. Now I've gotten IBM's lead test conductor in trouble, too.

"You're absolutely right, sir," adds Ed, ever the agreeable one.

The guard turns to Jake and before he can speak, Jake clarifies his position, "I'm just a NASA photographer. I don't even know those people."

Ed and I register shock, but with a mixture of disbelief and humor.

The security guard issues one more order: "You can go now. Mr. Goodwin, you need to escort this lady to her car and off the premises."

By the time I get back to the building in Cape Canaveral, Collins is pacing in the hallway, looking for me, waiting for an opportunity to exercise his managerial duties. I have made a huge mistake, and he is ready to pounce on it.

"I need to see you, now, in my office," he says.

"Sure," I answer meekly. Collins puffs on his cigarette as we walk in silence to his office. I know what is coming. I pick a chair, sit down, and wait for the cigarette and the lecture to begin.

"NASA Safety has called our security department to inform them about your violation. Nelson is also informed and so is Leon. Up around the IU in a miniskirt? You know better," his voice level rising with each sentence.

"And if that isn't bad enough you got our top test conductor cited, too. His manager called me and he's really pissed off. How do you think it looks for not one, but two of our people to receive violations—and then one of those is our test conductor?" His eyes dart back and forth, yet I expected as much, knowing he will milk this for all he can.

"Can I tell you my side of it?" I ask.

"This is serious. We just don't put ourselves in these kinds of predicaments. It was pointed out to me from Ed's manager, one of the top engineering guys for IBM, that we have never, do you hear me, under any circumstances, received a safety violation for this sort of thing. It looks bad for the whole facility...the whole damn company."

"I did have a reason. I knew what I was doing. I had a choice."

"That's even worse," he says.

"Just hear my side of it."

"All right, I'm listening."

"Jake, the NASA photographer, and I were shooting Ed Goodwin in the firing room when he happens to mention some astronauts are due to visit our people up around the IU level in five minutes. You know we don't get that many opportunities to get photos of the astronauts around the IU with our people. I didn't have time to change into a jumpsuit because the astronauts would have been gone by the time I got back. Ed just escorted us up there. I got him in some great photos with the astronauts right next to the IU. I'm sorry about the violations, especially Ed's. I never in a million years thought they'd ticket him. I thought I could get the photo and get out. "

Collins is quiet. He puffs on his cigarette, tilts back in his chair in deep thought.

"It was a moment to seize," I add. "A guy could have gone right up there without any questions and gotten the shots. I didn't want to be hindered from doing my job just because I'm a woman, who happens to be wearing a miniskirt."

"It's a safety rule, damn it, and you've got to respect the rules around here."

"It was a judgment call. You might have done the same thing. Just wait till you see the photos."

He pauses and takes another deep drag from his Camel cigarette. He is pondering it, thinking about it, but is he buying it? His eyes mellow, his body relaxes.

"They did take my badge away from me," I add.

"I know, and there's only one way to get it back."

"How?" I ask.

"You've been scheduled for Pad Evacuation Training."

"What does that entail?"

"For starters there's only been one other woman, a quality assurance inspector, who has taken the training so far. You'll learn about toxic pad gases and how to wear a facemask. The second day you'll learn how to egress the pad in the escape tube."

"Is this a rigorous thing? Why haven't more women taken this training?"

"It's limited specifically to those who must access the pad—those who really have business walking around next to the vehicle. I told them that your job requires you to interview key personnel who are assigned to the pad. You're scheduled for the next available class, which begins Monday. You can pick up your badge on the way out to the Safety building. It begins at 0700. And, yes, it is rigorous. You'll be reaching speeds up to 45 miles per hour when you shoot through the tube. But, you're an athletic woman, right?"

. . . .

CHAPTER 10

LET'S SLIDE

At home, when I want my girls to come home for dinner, I simply put my forefinger and thumb together, press on my tongue and whistle. It's a sound so penetrating that it can be heard indoors within a half-block radius. Not only do my kids recognize my whistle, but everyone else in the neighborhood does, too.

I whistle and my girls arrive home within five minutes, still in their Sunday clothes following Sunday school and brunch at the Eau Gallie Yacht Club.

"Get your tennis clothes on. We have a court reserved for 2:30. We'll leave in T minus 15 minutes." The girls squeal and run to their rooms to change. The phone rings and I walk to the family room to answer it.

"Hi, Babe," says Ed.

"What's up with you calling me on a Sunday?"

I don my overalls and pretend to be an engineer

"I've got some bad news. Someone saw us leave together last Friday and called my wife. She confronted me. We had a long talk. I confessed. But I lied about my true feelings for you. I told her you were just a one-night stand, a one-time flirtation. I said you didn't mean anything to me, and that I certainly don't mean anything to you. She was hurt by it all and cried. She asked me if I wanted to lose everything we had built together. I told her 'no.' I promised her I wouldn't see you again," his voice cracked and then added, "It's probably going to be the hardest thing I've ever done but I'm really going to put everything into it. I owe her that."

"Yes, you do, Ed. I understand. Believe me, I understand. It doesn't make it any easier or hurt any less, but I do understand. I've never been through anything like this before. The whole thing just got out of hand."

"I know, but it never had any future. You, with three kids and me—I hate kids. Where could it all go?"

"You're right. I want a good stepfather somewhere down the line. My kids deserve it."

"And you deserve a great guy. I'm going to say this just once—stash it away in your memory banks—I loved you, and I loved being with you."

"Thanks, Ed."

"Bye, Babe." I hang up the phone and dash into the bathroom, closing the door after me. I look at my reflection in the mirror and watch as the tears flood from my eyes. My chest heaves uncontrollably with sobbing. The pain burrows deep into my being, robbing my joy and replacing it with deep sadness and loss. The reality is, this affair ended like all affairs end. I realize the message behind the loss, but am absorbed in the pain of the moment.

"Mommy, we're ready," comes the sweet voice of Cathy, pulling me back to real-time.

"Okay, honey. We'll leave in T minus 5 minutes," I yell as I wash my face and put make-up on over my reddened nose. I cover my eyes with sunglasses and open the bathroom door thinking thank goodness I'll be busy this week. I've got pad evacuation training starting tomorrow, rehearsals, and lots of articles to write. I'll plan something to do with the girls every night. We'll have to start packing for camp this week. They'll leave Saturday.

I won't speak his name again. It's now in the past. He wasn't mine to begin with; I just borrowed him. I'll miss him for a while, but I'm going to let it go and move on. It's all right to hurt for a while—I will not dwell on it. It was never meant to be. There was something he said that made it much easier, too. Who wants a guy who hates children?

The next morning, I arrive at my desk at 6:30, before anyone else in the department. I take a plain piece of bond paper from my desk and insert it into my typewriter and begin typing: Man's happiness is intact, within, and is God-given, not dependent on people, places, or things.

I type it ten, twenty times, not to convince myself, but to combat the rush of negative thinking that floods my consciousness. I am alert as to how this kind of thinking creeps into my thoughts, masquerading as my own ideas; implying that my happiness is not complete without Ed around to supply it. I will have no part of it. I am determined to work through it.

Today is the beginning of pad evacuation training. I slept little last night between the break-up and fear of the class. Will I be able to complete this class? I don't want to make any more problems for IBM. I will focus my thoughts on more important things than feeling sorry for myself. I vow to make better choices for my happiness.

I arrive at 7 a.m. on the dot in front of the safety building, go to the receptionist and pick up my badge. It is a typical government building of concrete blocks, grey paint and metal furniture inside. I go down the hall to the training room and register at the desk with a large ruddy-skinned man with freckles and a crew cut of red hair.

"Sign the registration form, please, and leave your badge," he says.

I sign and hand him my badge.

"Oh, you're the one who got the safety violation. That's pretty serious business, wearing a miniskirt up there."

"I knew better. There were just extenuating circumstances. It's a long story."

"It always is," replied the safety inspector dryly.

About eight or nine men are sitting around the classroom, waiting for the class to begin.

"We'll begin the class as soon as the others join us. We've got three more coming from the MSOB," says ruddy man.

The MSOB is the Manned Spacecraft Operations Building. It's used for modification assembly and non-hazardous checkout of the spacecraft. It also houses the astronauts' quarters.

Ruddy man walks up to me and says, "The chief wants to talk with you privately before the class starts. Go down this hall, second door on the right."

I am imagining another chew-out as I listen to my heels click and echo. I soften my step as I approach the office where the sign reads: Daniel Doyle, Chief, NASA Security. I knock softly two times and waited for the go ahead to enter.

"Come on in," comes the voice behind the door.

"Good morning, sir. I'm Martha Croskeys," I say as I enter.

"Danny Doyle," he says as he rises and extends his hand. "I've heard a lot about you. Seems you've gotten yourself in some trouble."

"Yes sir, I have."

"Were you not aware of the rules establishing women who wear miniskirts on the platforms as safety hazards?

"Yes, sir. I was told about the rules. It's just that one of those lifetime opportunities came to get photos of the astronauts around our IU. I knew they would only be there a few minutes and I didn't have time to change. I stayed completely away from the sides of the platform," I explain. "I knew if I delayed I'd miss the opportunity. I was only up there for five minutes tops."

"A lot of things can happen in five minutes. We put these rules into effect for a purpose," he states with no smiles, no pardons, and no facial expressions whatsoever.

"What is it you do for IBM?"

"I'm a PR writer in the communications department."

"Mrs. Croskeys, the astronauts are not here at KSC solely to have their 'pitchers' taken by you. They have a much broader mission than other KSC employees, including you."

"Yes, sir," I agree as I nod my head.

"Now, I've come up with quite a class for you: A special class, different from any other egress training for civilians. I'm putting you in this class because I think it will make a point. I think you'll appreciate our astronauts a little more after these next couple of days. By the way, we've only had one other woman to take egress training, but you'll be the first in this special class. Now, go to the end of the hall. You'll find a bathroom. There's no ladies room; we just have one bathroom. Change your clothes into one of the white coveralls hanging up, store your personal items in a locker and then report to class."

"Yes, sir. Thank you, sir," I respond. Questions flood my thoughts: How did that other woman fare through this class? Did she panic? Will I panic? Will I be demoted back to being a secretary if I don't pass this class? Is my writing career over?

I reach the bathroom; open the door cautiously, hoping a man isn't using the facilities. The coveralls are hanging on a rack near the urinals. I pick out a size 'small' reasoning that all the sizes were meant for men, not women. I undress down to my bra and panties and step into the coverall and pull it up around me. I button eight or so buttons down the front and look into the mirror. The coveralls, made of cotton, have pockets in the front over each breast. The sleeves go all the way past my wrist so I fold them back. It looks pretty good, although a snug fit, especially around the hips. I reach into my large purse and pull out a pair of non-rubber soled, flat shoes to wear. I looked again in the mirror. Is it supposed to look this sexy, this form fitting?

My long, shoulder-length hair is down this morning. I take a brush out of my purse and brush my hair back and tie it with a rubber band into a ponytail. I open the door and walk back down the hall to the classroom where a movie screen and a projector are set up. All the men turn and stare at me as I enter the room. I'm sure these are the same uncouth men in the VAB who whistle and provide the catcalls. Ruddy man is behind the podium set up at the corner of the room.

"Just take a seat anywhere you'd like," he says as he motions me to the front. There are 14 desks set up. The desks are the kind that schools use, with a curved writing table in blond wood and a compartment under the seat for storage.

I look around the room and read a new Manned Flight Awareness poster. 'Take an Astronaut to Launch' it reads at the top, as a Johnny Hart cartoon character peers out from below the words. I turn my head and look at all the launch photos that surround the room. The door opens and in walks three more guys, dressed in orange coveralls. I look at the faces of the three men who will be my classmates and recognize the all-American, handsome faces, each with their own crew-cut as the trio of America's most recently assigned astronauts for future Apollo or Skylab missions. They come through the door in high spirits, smiling and laughing.

"Gentlemen, welcome, please take a seat," says ruddy man.

The astronauts waste no time finding the only woman in the room. The other guys in our group laugh as the astronauts choose to sit next to me, one to my right and the others to my left. I am smiling so hard it hurt my jaws.

"Let's begin by introducing ourselves, state your company affiliation and your position," says ruddy man who begins first. "My name is Ernest Banks and I'll be your instructor for the next couple of days. Now, let's begin with the first row," he says motioning to the astronaut next to me.

"Good morning, sir. Astronaut Bucky Horner, at your service. I used to be with the Air Force, flew jets in Nam. Now I'm with NASA, on my way to the moon."

He is around 34, 6 feet tall, salt and pepper hair, dark eyes, and muscular build. I notice the ring on his left hand.

"Nice to have you with us, Bucky," says Ernest.

"Nice to meet you Bucky," says one of the other astronauts, mocking.

"I'm Tom Evans, youngest astronaut in the entire astronaut crew, former Navy pilot. I also hold a degree in geology, which I guess NASA thought might come in handy."

It is obvious to me that these guys are pretty light-hearted about this class. No big deal to them, just a mandatory requirement to get out of the way. Compared to all the other rigorous training they must endure this is probably the easiest.

It's my turn; I rise from my seat, smile and say, "I'm Martha Croskeys, a writer from IBM. I received a safety violation for wearing a miniskirt around the IU level," several hoots and 'hollars' follow from the men. "I'm here as punishment but also to learn more about pad safety."

The last astronaut, rises, and says. "I'm Andy Scott. I'm the serious one in this group because I'm the senior officer. My job is to teach these two guys how to be astronauts...and believe me it is one hard job."

Andy, a Navy commander, is not only the senior member of the group but also the only one who has flown into space as one of the Gemini astronauts and aboard an earlier Apollo mission. He has light brown hair, green eyes and an inviting grin that takes over one side of his face when he smiles. He is athletic looking, yet slim, probably 36 - 38. Is he handsome? What astronaut is not handsome?

"Boy, it's getting deep in here," teases Bucky.

"That's commander to you," jokes Andy.

After going completely around the room with the rest of the guys chiming in with their professions as technicians and engineers, I realized the gaiety of the entire group and for the first time feel like this week could really be fun. I, too, have a mission: to keep up with these guys…all of them.

Ernie settles down and begins by saying, "Today, we're going to learn about the various fuels used by the different stages. These fuels are hazardous and if an accident occurs while you're on the pad, you'll have to don your gas masks for protection, or abandon the pad. We'll teach you how to accomplish both of these operations. There are many different fuels and gases used.

"If you don't remember anything else about this class, I hope you'll remember to run if you ever see a brown vapor escaping from the vehicle. The vapors should be white at all times. But we'll get into that more intensely in a minute.

"Oh yes, it's a good idea to take notes as a written test will be given in order to pass this class," says Ernie.

I glance to my left, then right and I'm the only one taking notes. I guess the astronauts know all this by heart. Ernie goes to the back of the room and clicks on the projector. "Please cut those lights to your right Bucky."

"Let's first look at this slide showing Launch Complex 39. This building right here is the LOX Facility, or liquid oxygen. The tank capacity is 900,000 gallons, stored at -297 degrees F. It has a transfer rate of 10,000 gallons per minute.

"Here's the H-P gas storage. This contains high-pressure gas including high-pressure nitrogen and helium gases for pressurizing and purging stages and ground support equipment. Eight hundred fifty thousand gallons of liquid hydrogen is stored here at a temperature of -423 degrees F.

"And at the RP-1 facility, which is here, we've got three 86,000 gallon tanks. The weight of our Saturn V fueled is 6,494,993 pounds. The explosive potential adds up to 1,000,000 pounds of TNT.

"Broken down by stages it goes like this: The first stage has 203,000 gallons of refined kerosene, RP-1, and 331,000 gallons of liquid oxygen in separate tanks. Clustered at the base of the stage are five engines, each 18-feet tall that consume all that fuel in 2 ½ minutes. These five engines burn oxygen at the same rate it is consumed by half a billion people, and fuel at the rate used by 3 million cars running simultaneously.

"The second stage is the most powerful hydrogen-fueled vehicle ever built. This is a 1,033,000-pound vehicle in which 90 percent of the weight is propellants. These tanks hold 267,700 gallons of super cold liquid hydrogen and 87,000 gallons of liquid oxygen, or LOX. Unlike air-breathing jet engines, rocket engines are self-contained. They must take along the necessary oxygen for combustion; otherwise they could not fire at all.

"The third stage weighs 260,000 pounds fueled. This stage's single engine fires when the vehicle approaches orbit. By firing more than two minutes, it boosts its speed to 17,400 miles an hour. It does this with 63,000 gallons of liquid hydrogen and 20,000 gallons of LOX.

"The service module, located here beneath the blunt end of the command module has a main rocket. This engine burns a fuel mixture of hydrazine and unsymmetrical dimethyl hydrazine, and an oxidizer of nitrogen tetroxide – the same propellants that are used in the Lunar Module.

"Now, we're going to view a movie that will show some of the various fuel procedures. It will also show you what the brown hazardous vapors look like." Ernie starts the projector and the narration begins.

"As the designers of the ill-fated Zeppelin Hindenburg could attest; hydrogen is a tricky, highly explosive gas. In liquid form it boils at minus 423 degrees F, and keeping it below that temperature in storage tanks and feed lines is difficult. Also, liquid hydrogen is very light, only seven percent as dense as water and requires..."

Out of my peripheral vision I can see Andy's head turn and look my way. Even with the blackout curtains over the windows, the light from the screen is enough to illuminate his face. I turn and find him smiling back at me.

We break for lunch, buying sandwiches from the "roach coach," a traveling food van. Back at our seats we are shown more movies of the fueling operation.

"Tomorrow," says Ernie, "you'll begin by taking your written fuel and gas tests. Then, you'll be required to put on your own gas mask and leave it on for at least 15 minutes. After that, we'll go over procedures for 'shooting the tube,' as we call it."

Ernie dismisses the class at 4:30. It is almost 5 o'clock by the time I get back to my office to check mail and messages. As I read through the pink telephone message slips, Warren sticks his head around the corner.

"How's it going in your class?"

"It's grueling...just grueling," I say grimacing as I speak. "A lot of technical gas names to learn and recognize. We have to pass a written test tomorrow so I've even got homework tonight. Tomorrow we have to put on gas masks and go down the tube too."

"How many in your class?"

"About a dozen—all men, and me."

"Well, hang in there," comes his advice.

I wasn't about to tell him the whole story—the fact that there are astronauts in my class and that I can hardly wait for tomorrow. Let him think that the class is punishment for me.

On the long trip to work the next morning, my thoughts are on my daughter, Cindy, who had once again awakened me with visions of a ghost cat in her room. What could this mysterious vision mean? What anxiety is triggering this illusion? I wonder if I should consult a professional.

The radio interrupts my thoughts and brings me the morning's news.

"The Apollo 10 astronauts appear in excellent condition following yesterday's splashdown in the Pacific after 31 orbits around the moon and a descent to within nine miles of the planned lunar landing site. The Soviet Union conducted underground tests yesterday…speculation from informed sources indicate that the Soviets are preparing for a major launch in the near future."

Everyone at the space center and in the space business across America is hoping the Russians aren't planning to get a jump on us with a shot to the moon. With just 50 days remaining until launch of Apollo 11, it could be a source of severe disappointment to come this close, only to lose the race to the moon.

With no need to stop at my office in Cape Canaveral, I cross Mather's Bridge at the southern tip of Merritt Island and enter KSC from State Road 3. I proceed straight to the one bathroom and change my clothes into the white coveralls. As I enter the classroom, Andy is in front of me in deep discussion with the other two astronauts.

"Hell, the liftoff for them was a rough ride with Pogo oscillation in both the first and second stages and a vibrating third stage as well. It still put them on such an accurate trajectory that they required only one tiny midcourse correction giving them 30 mph more to their velocity." He pauses and looks my way. "Good morning, Martha."

"Morning," echoes the other two.

"Are you ready for the rubber room?" asks Bucky.

"The rubber room? Is that a joke?" I ask.

"You'll find out," says Bucky.

I realize my whole attitude has changed from one of fear and concern to anticipation and excitement for the day's events. I am actually looking forward to shooting the tube since I will be doing it with these guys. Ernie enters the room and everyone scrambles for their seats.

"Good morning. I trust you're all rested and ready for today's adventure. We'll begin by looking at some slides depicting safety precautions for Pad 39." He walks over and turns off the lights as he begins the class.

"Pads A and B are virtually identical. They are roughly octagonal in shape. There's 8,716 feet between the two pads. Hardstand contains 68,000 cubic yards of concrete." He clicks the next slide onto the screen.

"The flame trench, shown here, is 42 feet deep, 450 feet long and 58 feet wide. The flame deflector weights 700 tons and is 41 feet high, 48 feet wide and 77 feet long.

"The industrial water system has a pumping rate of 45,000 gallons per minute. This sprays and flushes the mobile launcher and pad area during launches. It supplies five hydrants.

"Our pad safety crews are the ones who are systematically trained to respond to pad fires. Here's a shot of them at work."

Once again, I feel Andy's gaze on me. I turn and our eyes meet. We hold our gaze until both of us smile.

"Once a tank is filled with hydrogen it has to be inspected for leaks and this is a tricky procedure. A jet of escaping hydrogen is apt to combine with oxygen in the air and burn, but in daylight the flame is invisible. McDonnell-Douglas uses infrared cameras on its test stands to detect hydrogen leaks, but even the cameras have blind spots, so they bring in men around the scaffolding, wearing protective clothes and holding brooms out in front of them. If a broom suddenly burst into flames, there's a leak."

I continue to take notes for another hour, many in shorthand. Still there is no note taking from any of crew but they do give their respect and attention to Ernie.

"We're going to perform our gas mask certification now," announces Ernie, as he flicks the light switch back on. "Please come up and choose your gas mask." The gas masks are sitting on the table in the front of the class. I choose mine and slip it over the front of my head and pull it back with my right hand. I adjust the sides and take a deep breath to draw the air. The trio waste no time, having their masks on well before me, or anyone else in the class.

"You look like a giant ant," says Andy to me in a muffled voice.

"I'd like to wear this to my management meetings when everyone smokes but me."

My claustrophobia vanishes as 'the guys' continued to put me at ease with their friendliness and playful attitude. Ernie examines each person to make sure they have the proper seals and the masks are securely fitted around their faces. After the required 15 minutes, he instructs us to remove them. Red marks on our faces reveal the tightness of the masks. I give a sigh of relief, hoping I never have to use one.

"There's nothing like the real thing...fresh air," says Bucky.

"Please take your seats for the written part of the test," says Ernie. "You'll have 20 minutes to complete the questions. All questions are in the form of either multiple choice or true or false. You must pass this test in order to proceed with the egress training."

I stayed up late last night, studying and even learning to correctly spell all the various gases and fuels. I am confident and prepared. Everyone finishes before the allotted time but I choose to go back and recheck my answers. After 20 minutes Ernie announces that time is up.

"Please hand in your papers. While I am grading your papers, you can be excused for your lunch break. The food van should be parked outside by now."

Bucky opens the door and the rest of us leave the building squinting as we emerge into the brightness of the Florida sun. The roach coach sits in front, waiting for us just as Ernie has promised. I order the ready-made ham and cheese on rye with mustard and a Coke to drink. Seems the three crew members, sitting beside me on the concrete table and bench, are determined to stay with the only woman in the group, lucky me.

Andy speaks first: "So, Martha, do you have a family? Where do you live?"

"I'm divorced with three daughters. I live about an hour south of here in a small beach community called Indialantic. How about you guys?"

"We all live in Houston with our wives. I've got one son," says Andy.

"I've got a son and a daughter," says Tom.

"How long are you here at the Cape?" I ask.

"It depends. We can stay for weeks, or come and go. We fly our own T-38's into Patrick Air Force Base. It all depends on how much training we've got to do and when we can schedule time on the simulators," explains Andy.

"Did you guys pass our test?" I ask.

They all shook their heads. "We've had this kind of training along the way in our careers but we still have to be certified here," says Tom.

"The Apollo 10 crew made it down safely yesterday. It was a remarkably trouble-free mission."

"Those guys, you know, Cernan, Stafford and Young, were the crew originally scheduled to land on the moon. But their vehicles had a lot of delays forcing NASA to make changes that required Apollo 10 to do the 'fly around the moon.' This changed the landing craft from Apollo 10 to 11," reveals Andy. "They got to carry real bread on their flight and make their own chicken salad sandwiches."

"Tell the whole truth. The bread had been flushed with nitrogen to keep it fresh, and the chicken salad was a prepared spread," says Tom. "It might have been the first official use of bread, but I remember John Young pulled a kosher, corned-beef sandwich from his pocket and offered it to Gus Grissom during their Gemini 3 flight."

"Yeah…the remains of that sandwich were enshrined in a plastic case on his desk, along with an official reprimand," adds Andy. "Of course, water was the real problem on that flight. It was over-chlorinated and the entire supply had to be dumped overboard. They had to resort to using the water from the fuel cells."

"I didn't know that water was drinkable," I say.

"Sure, the fuel cells produce water as a by-product when they generate electricity from liquid oxygen and liquid hydrogen."

"What are you doing in this class, Martha?" asks Tom, as the others turn their heads in unison to catch my answer.

"It's sort of embarrassing. I was just trying to get a great photo of our test conductor with Shepard. I didn't have time to change into the coveralls."

"I didn't know you couldn't wear miniskirts up there. What's the reason?" asks Bucky.

"They claim that all the guys looking up at the skirts from below could lose their concentration and fall. Actually, I think Mr. Doyle, the head of Safety, put me in this class with you all to give me a greater appreciation for our valuable cargo."

"Well, I sure want to be appreciated," smiles Andy.

"Do you think you'll be able to shoot the tube? You won't chicken out, will you? We'll be going pretty fast," says Tom.

"Hey, I'm athletic. I'm a tomboy from way back. I even quarterbacked our junior girl's touch football team to a win. I can beat most guys at arm wrestling and I'm an excellent tennis player. You're looking at the IBM men's tennis champion for the past two years."

"How'd you manage that one?"

"There was no women's division, so I talked them into having an open tournament so I could play. Don't worry about me. I'm coordinated and in great shape."

"I'll agree with that statement," says Andy. "Well, I think it time to join the others."

We dispose of our bottles and paper in a nearby trash container and head indoors.

As soon as we sit down in our chairs, Bucky leans over to me to ask, "What if you don't pass this class?"

Andy, overhearing his question, shoots back, "What if you don't pass, Bucky?"

Ernie enters the room with a smile. "I have good news. You all passed the written test. Five of you have perfect scores and the rest of you missed from two to eight questions. Andy, Tom, Bucky, Virgil and Martha have perfect scores. We'll now proceed to the egress part of the class."

I can't stop grinning. I have a perfect score. So far, I'm definitely keeping up. Ernie begins his instructions: "The emergency egress system has a

200-foot long escape tube, or slide, which runs from the top of the mobile launcher platform to the blast resistant room, also know as the 'rubber room.' It got this name because it has six inches of rubber insulation on the floors, walls and ceilings. It is important when you begin your descent that you allow the lighter-weighted persons to go last; otherwise, the heavier people will overtake the lighter ones on the way down since the heavier people will travel faster. Also, please count off ten full seconds in-between each person's descent.

"Going down the tube, you should assume a sitting position with the palms of your hands facing each other, placed between your knees. This position allows you to transgress the many winding turns with speeds up to 45 miles per hour. Do not wear any shoes, as we do not want anything to impede your speed. Keep your socks on. The 200-foot chute will take you into the blast room where there are 20 chairs, safety harnesses and survival gear for 24 hours, including food and water. The blast room, or rubber room, can cut a 75 G force to only 4 G's as you enter the room.

"Another method of escape from the pad in case of fire is the cab on a guide wire from the 320 foot level to revetment 2,500 feet away. We will not go into that today. That's another class entirely.

"You'll come out into the rubber room, facing a rubber wall. Your impact against this wall can be braced with your feet, as you will lose velocity by the time you hit the wall. Let's go to the back of the room and sit on the floor."

We follow Ernie as he sits down on the floor in a perfect chute position. "Let's now assume the sitting position required for the tube. All you have to do is go with the flow. Put your hands between your knees, lean to the left or lean to the right as you go around he curves. Keep your balance at all times and look straight ahead of your feet."

I get into my position and immediately Andy looks my way. "Stretch out a little more," he says.

Ernie comes by each student and tilts us one way, then the other. "Do not take your hands free from inside your knees at any time. If you do this right, it's a fun trip down; if you don't, you could be badly hurt." He looks at his watch and speaks again. "A bus should be out front for us now to take us to the pad. If you'll follow me, we'll get on our way."

As we board the bus, Bucky speaks, "Let's sing camp songs."

"You did very well on your test," says Andy as we find our seats.

"You did good on yours as well," I answer. "You probably didn't have to stay up all night studying for it either."

"Right again."

We drive the five miles to perimeter road and around the pad, past the burn pond and onto Road F. "Visitors are allowed today, even though the vehicle is on the pad. After it's fueled is a different story. Then, only personnel whose jobs take place directly on the pad are allowed in this area," explains Ernie.

We leave the bus and walk a short distance to the mobile launcher. It seemed big before, but now as I look up at the massive structure in front of me, I feel like an ant at the base of an oak tree. My heart is pounding as we walk up the steep steps onto the base of the ML and enter an enclosed room.

"This is the entrance," says Ernie, as he points down to an open area and lifts the hatch. "When you get below, you'll have to remain down there until you hear the 'all clear' sound which occurs in about 15 minutes. Okay, we're ready when you are."

"Martha, why don't you go first?" asks Andy, testing my knowledge of vital information that was reported in the class.

"I heard that part. The heavier people are supposed to go first. I'm going last. You wouldn't want to run over me, would you, Andy?" He lifts his eyebrows and turns his head to ponder the question.

"Okay, we'll go first and show you how it's done. We'll be down there to help you when you hit bottom. It helps to yell something like 'Geronimo.'"

We discard our shoes into a plastic bag and leave them with Ernie. Andy, true to form, is the first one down, yelling 'Geronimo' until his voice fades and can be heard no more. Bucky counts off ten seconds and pushes off, singing the Air Force fight song. "Off we go into the wild blue yonder...."

Tom waits his ten seconds, pushing off yelling, "Open the hatch, and pour me in...."

I wait for the rest of the class to go down. I am alone on top of the pad, counting off my ten seconds by taking in a view that I'll probably never see again. Here I am on the top of a Saturn V vehicle, in fact, the one that will carry our astronauts to the moon, Apollo 11. Five, one thousand, 4, one thousand—I search the area and find the VAB, look to the ocean—3, one thousand, 2, one thousand, 1, one thousand...and I push off yelling, "Oh, shit!" Half way down, I realize I am having fun. I twist and turn with every curve, keeping my hands between my knees, my gaze above my feet. It is just as fast as Ernie promised. I catapult into the rubber room, still in my seated position, with the wall coming straight at me. I put up my legs to brace. Just as I hit, Andy is there to help me up.

"Nice landing," he says as he helps me to a standing position.

I raise both hands above me, clasping my fists. "I did it, I can't believe what I just did! That was so much fun. I'd do it again in a second." The other guys come over to extend their congratulations to me. I feel so honored.

The rubber room is about the size of a small two-bedroom house. The room is just as Ernie described it, six inches of rubber upholstered with green vinyl. The only illumination in the room is two red lights, with protective wire baskets. The combination of the green room and the red lights gives off a surrealistic effect. The rest of the guys in the class mingle together, finding seats, to await the all-clear sign.

"Isn't it neat down here?" asks Tom. "A whole world to ourselves."

"Come look at the kitchen," says Bucky as I follow with childlike anticipation for each new revelation. "The cabinets are stocked with food, water and first aid supplies. The entire room is equipped with a separate generator, producing its own air supply system."

"They've certainly thought of everything," I say as my eyes search out every inch.

"This door leads to the crawl tunnel, which is used if the power shuts off, or we're stranded down here for more than 24 hours. We can crawl on our hands and knees through this tunnel for a thousand feet to the other side of the pad. I did it once and it was filled with debris, rats and snakes," says Andy.

"What are we supposed to do for 15 minutes down here?" I ask.

"Good question. You probably think we can do or say anything we want to down here, as private as it seems. But, look again. We're being monitored by cameras," he says as he points to the lens. "The only thing allowable in this light is to just talk. Somebody pick a subject," suggests Tom, as we find a chair and sit down.

"Tennis," says Bucky. "Martha likes tennis."

"All right. Who's going to win the U.S. Open this year now that the open era is in its second year?" asks Andy.

"I'll pick John Newcomb and Billie Jean," I say.

"Nah, Laver and Court will win," adds Tom. After a long pause with no other comments, Tom concludes, "Well, so much for our tennis expertise."

"Seen any good movies lately?" asks Bucky.

"I liked *Rhinestone Cowboy*, although it was depressing," I say.

"I liked *True Grit* with John Wayne. That was a good movie," says Bucky.

"How 'bout *Butch Cassidy and the Sundance Kid*? I like that one," adds Tom.

"I love Robert Redford," I confess. After another long pause I make a bold decision. "Let me ask you guys a real question."

"Oh, oh, the writer in her emerges to seize this golden opportunity," teases Andy.

"No, off the record. Don't you guys ever get scared about what's ahead? You seem so cavalier, so light-hearted."

Andy speaks first: "We don't have time to get scared. We're training every minute, which alone gives you the confidence and knowledge to do your job. When we're in flight there are just too many functions to perform to even think about getting scared. We're totally absorbed in each moment, busy every second."

"There have been guys up there who panicked, but no one, at least no one on the outside, heard about it," adds Tom.

"I'm more afraid of these two guys than I am of space flight," jokes Bucky.

"What if you are made part of a crew and there's a personality problem with one of the other guys?" I ask.

"That's happened before, too. The mission has to take precedence over any personal feelings," explains Andy.

"What do you think will happen down the road for you guys, say in 40 or 50 years. What will you be doing?"

"I hope I'm the chairman of the board of some public company," says Andy.

"I want to still be involved in the space program, maybe director of NASA," says Tom.

"I want to be retired, babysitting my grandchildren," adds Bucky.

"What about you, Martha, what do you think you'll be doing then?" asks Andy.

"I'll be going to the movie premiere of my best-selling novel." A siren blasts through the air, red lights flash, my eyes widen with a quizzical expression.

"It's okay," says Bucky. "It's just the all-clear signal. When it stops, the real lights will come on and we'll be able to take the elevator up."

Once atop, Ernie greets us with our bag of shoes. We board the van and head back to the security building, everyone laughing and joking with one another. Ernie wraps it up by saying, "That concludes our time with you. We hope these instructions will never have to be used. Thank you for attending."

As we depart the bus, Andy speaks first. "It's been fun. It's always nice to have a little change of pace. We don't get to be around too many women, especially good looking women."

"It's an adventure I'll always remember. Good luck with your training and on your mission. You'll all be in my prayers." I offer my hand, but Andy grabs me and gives me a big hug; Bucky and Tom follow with hugs of their own.

.

. . . .

CHAPTER 11

IBM'S CONTROL CENTER...AND APOLLO 11 DINNER

ocated in the Cape Canaveral administration building, down the hall from my office, is one huge room dedicated as the IBM Control or Conference Center. The room is filled with communications equipment linked to KSC. Also, we use this room for visitors to show slides and movies on the pull-down screen; this is where Nelson holds his staff meetings every Monday morning at7:30 a.m. Each key manager reports the status of his section's part in the overall mission. Collins then sends reports to division and corporate. Besides the in-house reports, he also sends updates to NASA, who then issues status reports for the entire mission that are then relayed to all contractors every week. The worst thing that can occur at one of these meeting is for Nelson to find out that IBM is responsible for not meeting a deadline, or that some infraction has occurred.

In the past, Warren has always sent Tom to the meetings as a way of finding out what stories we should be addressing. Today, he is sending

The original Missiletown Pipers include: Bob Ehrhardt, Pete Theobald, Mary Jo Sloan, Ralph Cunningham, Martha Lemasters, Diane Baker, Sara McIntire, Janet Caron, Marion Bucko and Don Cremins...and pianist Missy Klinzing

me. It is a big honor to sit in on one of these meetings. There are no female managers here at the IBM facility at present so it is rare that a woman attends.

I arrive early and chat with Pete Theobald, one of our chorus members. Pete is a fun guy with a great sense of humor. He's also a super sharp engineer. I take my seat in the far back, knowing that the top managers will be filling the room. I sit quietly and observe as Nelson steps to the podium and pushes a button. A huge electronic curtain pulls back revealing Bart charts, launch countdown schedules, budget charts and a huge organization chart.

The majestic Saturn in Highbay 3 (NASA)

"Good morning, gentlemen. I'd like to acknowledge the presence of Martha Croskeys, who is sitting in on today's meeting. We only have a few days until liftoff. I cannot express how crucial, how critical, these days ahead are for us. It is imperative that we stay on schedule and

The 363 foot high Apollo/Saturn V vehicle leaves the VAB (NASA)

remain error-free, and alert to any problems. With that said, we'll begin with our status reports. IU Mechanical and Electrical Systems Engineering, Bob Ehrhardt."

Bob stands up and approaches the Bart chart, the largest chart on the boards. "We expect to be online with the projected commencement of the count at T-28 hours. We're anticipating no problems, no holds, no delays. All tests are positive and we expect to proceed without any incidents."

"Good news, Bob, thank you. Next is Ground Network Systems Engineering, Dave Dowd."

"We are on schedule and report no problems," says Dowd.

"Great," says Nelson. "Let's hear from Ground Computer Systems Engineering and DEE-6 & CDC Systems Engineering, Pete Theobald."

"Well, we've got a problem," begins Pete. Even as he speaks these words that Nelson never wants to hear, Nelson reacts immediately. His left hand opens widely, takes the piece of paper directly under it and slowly starts to squeeze it into a wad, crumpling it into the palm of his hand. He takes the paper from his left hand into his right hand and hurls it across the room. All eyes in the room follow that piece of paper until it finds its resting place.

Without missing a beat, Pete continues with his report, his right hand mimicking the actions that Nelson has taken with the wadded up paper. "We've had more than six people out with the flu, we have tests to run, installations to perform, but we can't do it without the proper manpower." His hand is now wadding up the paper completely. All eyes are riveted on Pete's piece of paper.

"These men are in one-of-a-kind positions, each trained specifically for their own system. We have backup engineers in place, but the ones who are sick are scheduled for Apollo 11. Illness is something we cannot compensate for, nor anticipate." He takes the piece of wadded paper ball and throws it at the same place that Nelson has thrown his. A hush goes throughout the whole room. No one dares to speak. I am spellbound, wondering what will happen next.

Several minutes go by in silence, then a smile spreads across Nelson's face and he asks, "Well, how long do you think your men will be out, Pete?" Everyone relaxes and smiles for we know from Nelson's tone of voice that he has taken the mimicry with good-natured humor.

"Just a few more days, sir. We'll work around the clock and make up for the lost time. We should be back online next week."

"Very well. Let's hear from Measuring and TM Systems engineering," but before he can call on Jim Tompkins, the phone rings. Nelson immediately picks it up. It's a rule that only emergency calls are put through during the meetings.

"Martha, you have an emergency call from home." I know the girls are home for a teachers' workday. I take the call in front of the whole table of IBM's most important executives, the ones who make all the decisions, who run the show for IBM. I pray that there is not an accident, or sickness.

"Martha Croskeys," I say as I answer the phone in front of the entire world.

"Hi Mommie," says Cathy, "Can I split a coke with Curran?"

"Why, yes, of course," I answer, trying to keep it sounding professional.

"Cindy's got a big surprise for you when you get home," she adds.

"Very well," I answer. "I'll see you later, then." I hang up; grateful the conversation wasn't on the speakerphone for all to hear.

"Everything all right?" asks Nelson.

"Yes. I have another important job; that of Mother, which is also demanding. Sorry for the interruption," I suspect that if it had been one of the guys, Nelson might not have been so understanding.

Following the meeting, I return to my office to write up a schedule of activities for possible articles. Later, as I take the list out of my typewriter and head to Warren's office, I see Gail in the hall. She smiles and comes over to speak.

"How's everything going?"

"Couldn't be better," she replies, as I put my hand on her shoulder.

"That's just wonderful. I'm so glad everything's working out for you." I notice Warren down the hall and cut my pleasantries off. "I've got to catch Warren. We'll talk more later, Gail."

I walk into his office and hand him the list of story possibilities.

"Sit down, I'd like to tell you something." I sit down in the nearest chair, right in front of his desk. I notice the ashtray is filled with at least a pack of cigarette butts, as he works on another out of the corner of his mouth. He squints his small eyes, takes a deep puff, blows the smoke my way, and places the cigarette in the tray in front of me. He's not handsome by any stretch of the imagination. He is an average-looking kind of guy. He has medium-length black hair that is fertilized regularly by Vaseline hair tonic that provides a shine to his hair. I've never thought of him in terms of 'the opposite sex' nor friend. He is my manager, an authority figure whom I report to at work. I neither fear him nor allow him to intimidate me. I am confident about the quality and quantity of my work and I have the appraisals to back up that confidence.

"I want to talk to you about something that's bothering me," he begins. "I've noticed something on more than one occasion that's, well, really unprofessional. You're…. you're too physical with people. You have to touch everyone you talk to." I quickly recall touching Gail on the shoulder just a few minutes ago.

"What does that have to do with my performance as a writer?"

"You can't talk to people without touching them. As soon as you walk up to them, you're touching them. You touch them on their shoulders, on their backs. You're just a 'toucher,'" he says as if I am some sort of sex predator. "This shouldn't happen in the work place. I'm just saying, you need to cool it with all the physical touching."

I can't believe what I am hearing. "Is this an IBM rule, this 'no contact' thing?" I ask, as I look him right in the eyes.

"Not a written rule, no."

"I don't believe there's a category on my appraisal for touching. This subject that you've pulled out of the air doesn't fall within any manager's jurisdiction. I'm going to forget you said this to me; and you'd better be thankful that I don't write a Speak Up!" I say, as I stand to leave.

"Sit down," he says firmly. "Your actions are my business."

"I'm not even going to discuss this with you. Just back off," I say, turning to walk out of his office, biting my lip, holding back what I really want to say. I've gotten tougher, that's for sure. I've learned to take up for what's right and look the other way on things like this. Still, when I get inside my office I throw my steno pad across the small room, sit down, and count backwards from 10.

Warren is no different from other male managers. For some reason they think they should be controlling every aspect of one's job, especially, it seems, when the employee is a woman.

At lunch I represent IBM by attending the monthly meeting for the Cape Kennedy PR Association, held upstairs at Ramon's Restaurant. The members consist of representatives from all NASA contractors, as well as other local business and college reps. As the only woman present, and definitely the only one who will not imbibe alcohol, I sit next to Patrick Smith, the PR rep from Brevard Community College, a 'gentleman and a scholar.' Patrick has high hopes to someday finish his novel that he has been working on. He gives me a brief update. Each month a different member of the association is responsible for securing the speaker, or movie. As we are served our lunch, music begins and the lights dim.

Suddenly, a scantily clad woman emerges, performing a sensuous dance. "Okay, that's something new," I say to Patrick. "We've never had a dancer before."

"I think she's more than a dancer," says Patrick. Soon, she is stripping down to her thong. I keep eating my lunch, concentrating on cutting my chicken. I finish my last bites and get up to leave. I wonder whose bright idea this was as I start out the door: North American, Boeing, McDonnell-Douglas, GE. Which contractor rep thought this a good idea? I wave my goodbyes to the group.

Later, as I drive into my garage at home, I remember the message that Cathy told me on the phone, that Cindy has a surprise for me. I can hardly wait to see it. She has probably drawn a card for me, or made something. I walk in the house and am greeted by three glowing, smiling faces eager to show me my surprise. Cindy takes my hand and guides me to the hall where she shows me with all her pride her masterpiece. I look up to see the entire hall wall filled with lipstick pictures of everything imaginable...cats, dogs, and words of love. "I love you, Mommie."

My heart sinks knowing that all my lipstick has been used for this montage and that it will take at least three coats of paint to get it off. I look down at my beautiful, sweet daughters and say the only words that are appropriate, "What a beautiful painting. Did you do this all by yourself?"

"No, Cathy helped me."

"I told them not to do it," says the oldest, Curran.

"Well, it's just the most beautiful thing I've ever seen. I love it so much. Thank you. I love you all so much."

"We love you, Mommie."

"Just don't brush up against it tonight. You'll get lipstick all over you, okay?"

As the days roll by, I tell no one about my marvelous adventure with Andy, Tom and Bucky, and for that matter my affair with Ed. I have a very private side that I don't share with anyone while I learn to decipher life's mysteries. My thoughts are my sanctuary where I cherish my precious memories that are now bouncing between my last goodbyes with Ed to the joyful egress class with the astronauts, to the anticipation of tonight's facility dinner show for Apollo 11.

I walk to the cafeteria and punch a button from the machine and a carton of milk falls down. I never drink coffee, no matter how early I rise, or how late I work. As I unfold the top of the cartoon, Jo walks up.

"Tonight's the night," she says.

"I can hardly wait. I think we've got our best show ever," I reply.

"I love the skit you wrote. Everyone will get a kick out of it."

"Is your hubby going to make it?" Jo's husband has caused quite a stir when he was fired as a quality control inspector for North American for sleeping on the job. He now works in the parts department for a local car dealer.

"No, he won't be there; he'll stay home with the kids," she says as we pull up chairs at a nearby table.

"How's it going with him?"

"He's on medication but his mood swings are so unpredictable and his temper seems uncontrollable. It scares me to death. I just want out. I don't love him any more. I've lost respect. I can barely stand to sleep in the same bed with him, and then I keep one eye open."

"What are you going to do? This is no way to live."

"I don't know. I wish I were stronger, like you. I envy your strength in going ahead with your divorce. I think he even resents my singing, the spotlight it gives me. Singing in our group has given me friends, too."

"You've got a good job, you could make it without him, you know."

"There's too much pressure here at work without adding more at home."

"Let me know if there's anything I can do," I say as I close up my milk carton and rise. I never hesitate to get involved if my friends need me but I have two rules that I try to abide by: Not to judge and not to give advice, just give information and let them choose their own path.

"Are you going all the way home after work and then coming back?" asks Jo.

"No, I've brought everything with me. I've got to run through Nelson's speech with him right after work, then I'll go directly to the Hilton." I start down the hall and recognize my phone ringing so I rush to my office, just on the other side of the cafeteria.

"IBM Communications, Martha Croskeys," I say.

"Martha, it's Kevin Griggs. I need a personal favor."

I wait a few seconds to absorb his request. Kevin is one of my good friends from the chorus and he's never asked for a favor before. "What is it, Kevin, I'll do what I can, you know that."

"I left my car at a friend's house last night. I just need you to pick it up."

"A friend's house. How friendly, Kevin?"

"As friendly as it gets. Her old man came home right when I was there. I just made it out the back door with my shoes and clothes in my hand. I ran the half block home. The problem is my car is parked in front of her house and I'm afraid he'll catch me if he sees me. He might be lying in wait. Can you meet me over here and get my car for me? He won't think anything about it if a woman picks up the car. He'll probably think you're a Mary Kay lady."

"I don't know, this sounds like it's dangerous. This is your problem Kevin, not mine."

"What if I offer you 15 Florida lobsters that I just snagged from Sunday's dive?"

"Make it 20 lobsters and I'll do it on my lunch hour...in about 30 minutes."

The next time I see Kevin, he's standing in his garage as I pull my car to a stop, put it in park and shut off the engine.

"Did you call in sick today?" I ask.

"I had a dental appointment this morning."

"Where's your car?"

"Right down there," he points down the street. "It's that '69 white Chevy with the canvas top, parked in front of the white house with the black trim."

"Isn't that Waldo's house?"

"It is."

"You're having an affair with Waldo's wife? That bully?" I ask in amazement, realizing this situation has just gotten a lot more dangerous than originally thought.

"I felt sorry for her."

"Yeah? Well, we'll all feel sorry for you if he catches you. Let me understand this correctly. You want me to go down to Waldo's house, a man whom you describe as a raving madman, and rescue your car. What if he has the sights of his gun aimed that way? What if he's put a bomb in your car? This puts a different light on everything. Now we're talking about hazardous duty. This looks like a 24-lobster-favor now."

"They're yours—heads cut off—and frozen. Here are the keys. When you get the car, drive it around the block. I'll meet you there and bring you back to your car."

"Okay." I take the keys and slowly walk to the parked car in front of Waldo's house. Why in the world would he park right in front? I glance at the windows of Waldo's house to see if anyone peers out, but I can't see anything. I approach the car, looking to my left, then right, and open the door. As soon as I enter, I lock all the doors and adjust the rear-view mirror. I put the keys in the ignition and turn it on. No bomb. The Chevy engine kicks over and starts easily. I nudge it into gear, drive around the block and pick up Kevin.

"Looks like you're in the clear," I say.

"I'll drop your lobsters off before you leave work on Monday."

"Okay. See you tonight."

The much-awaited dinner is held right across the street from our building at the Cape Kennedy Hilton, the newest hotel in the area, and the only one with a huge convention-type room. Approximately 1200 employees and their spouses will be treated to dinner, speeches, songs and a special skit.

After the invocation, the band plays music through dinner until Nelson takes the stage and starts to speak from the podium. He smiles and waits for the room to quiet.

"Good evening. We're glad you're here tonight. This is a very special evening, one to reminisce, to celebrate and to look ahead. Before we begin our program, I'd like to introduce some of our guests. Our division president, Mr. John Jackson." Nelson waits for the polite applause to stop.

"Next, it is my great pleasure to welcome and introduce Apollo astronauts Andy Scott, Tom Evans and Bucky Horner." A thunderous applause is followed by a standing ovation. Backstage, I'm waiting behind the curtains in the front row of the chorus line. I turn to Jo and say, "I didn't know they'd be here."

"We weren't sure which astronauts NASA would send until the last minute," says Jo.

"After the applause quiets down, Nelson again turns to the mike and continues. "We've put together a special program, performed by your co-workers, that I'm sure you're going to enjoy. So without further to do, sit back and enjoy the show."

The heavy curtain starts opening to either side, revealing the chorus against the backdrop of the Saturn V painted by members of our art department, across a huge canvas, sitting on the pad. Leon has made only a few changes in the last weeks of rehearsals: the most significant is the opening, inspired by the Vietnam situation. As the curtain comes to a stop, Leon takes his place in the orchestra pit. The eyes of the entire chorus rivet on him as he holds up his baton, and lets it down.

Let there be peace on earth and let it begin with me.

Let there be peace on earth, the peace that was meant to be...

As I sing I search the audience for my buddies. There at the main table, sitting with the division president, are Andy, Tom and Bucky. I look right at them, smile and nod my head. They acknowledge me and smile back.

Next, we sing This is my County, followed by the IBM rally song, *Ever Onward*, the Beatles' *Let it Be* and *Hey, Jude*. The solos follow, Jo sings *A Time for Us*. Ralph, dressed in a dashiki, belts out *Up, Up and Away*, which brings smiles to the faces in the audience.

The skit I wrote follows. I am dressed in a mini-dress of silver lame, with silver boots. Kevin and I will perform as husband and wife, coming home from a long day at the office—on Mars. We discuss the day's activities. Then I mysteriously have a malfunction. When he turns me around there is a big IBM logo on my back, revealing that I am an IBM android, programmed to answer every need of my husband. He winds me up and says, "Doesn't IBM think of everything?"

As we bow to the applause, my eyes again find Andy, who is smiling and vigorously applauding. Nelson signals Andy, Tom and Bucky to the stage. After presenting them with a plaque, he turns the mike over to them. Andy, as protocol dictates, speaks first.

"I've heard a lot of good things about how hard you people work and how dedicated you are. Now, we've seen that you're a pretty talented group as well. As you might know, the Apollo 11 crew is confined to quarters. They've been training hard. They told us to be sure to say 'Thank you' to each and every one of you. So, on their behalf now, and on behalf of our future missions, thank you, and keep up the good work."

I am still in the wings, but I recognize Andy's voice over the PA system. He is so cool, so gracious, and I can call him 'friend.' Tom is next on the podium.

"We've really enjoyed the show tonight and being among our team members. Just keep up your great support, and thanks for inviting us."

Bucky follows with his words: "You IBMers are a hard working, dedicated team, and you know how to have fun, too. Keep it up and thanks for a great evening." As the astronauts take their seats, Nelson organizes his papers for his speech. Once again he waits for and receives complete silence in the huge auditorium.

"I believe that President Kennedy was convinced that a second-rate, second-place space effort was inconsistent with this country's role. America has assembled the greatest team of all time to meet his goal. And…Kennedy was right, it has been expensive and it has been difficult. Hard work, the kind that keeps you up at night, headaches, even some heartaches, have gone into this massive effort. The final countdown for our liftoff will begin shortly. As you go about performing your tasks over the next days and hours, your duties, your work, will be etched in memory for years to come—most likely for our lifetimes.

"We are at this time and place, taking part in magnificent history. All that we do in the days remaining will help make Apollo 11's journey to another planet not only possible, but also safe. At this crucial point, I ask each of you to renew your dedication to error-free performances—a personal rededication to pride in workmanship. We have established unprecedented standards for high quality. This critical mission, with the world's eyes upon us, demands that we maintain this level of commitment.

"I want to take this opportunity to thank each one of you for your personal sacrifices—and I know there have been many. I know you've worked long hours that have kept you from your families. I know you've had pressures that the average person could never even imagine. I know that you've faced personal crises that have had to be put aside for the sake of the mission. I know the strength of this team that sits before me. You are a team I am immensely proud of, a team that has fulfilled my expectations, a team I would trust my life to. And three men—three astronauts—will be doing so shortly.

"This is an epochal event—a turning point in the history of our universe—and every one of us can walk a little taller, be a little prouder, knowing that with your help Americans will finally touch the moon, walk on it, sample it, expose their human vision and earthly sensors to its strange barrenness, and come home safely to show and tell the world about it.

"The lunar landing will be the coming of age for manned space flight. This team has put its finest effort into this mission and I am confident Apollo 11 will fulfill our highest hopes and expectations.

"For your personal contributions to this mission, I thank you one and all. And now, Godspeed Apollo 11."

A loud standing ovation, led by the astronauts, fills the room. The curtains again open to the entire chorus in place as we begin singing, "*Oh, beautiful, for spacious skies, for amber waves of grain....*" This is followed by *The Battle Hymn of the Republic*. At one point, the entire audience stands, hands entwined, singing and swaying with us. At the conclusion of the song, everyone lifts their hands over their heads with a triumphant yell.

I really didn't expect such an emotional reaction. There is hardly a dry eye in the room. A feeling of jubilation for the songs, the skit and the speeches, that hit the mark, fills the banquet room. When the applause finally stops, everyone spontaneously hugs one another both in the audience and on stage. Nelson returns to the mike, thanks everyone for attending and says, "Good night."

I am reeling, grinning from ear to ear. Everyone is congratulating one another on stage when I turn and see Andy coming toward me, Tom and Bucky by his side. I walk toward him.

"What a great job you guys did," says Andy.

"Terrific show," adds Tom.

"Really good, and lots of fun," says Bucky.

"Thanks," I say, as they all take turns hugging me. "I was so surprised to see you in the audience."

"You hadn't heard we were coming?" asks Andy.

"No, not at all. We just knew some astronauts would be attending." Jo walks up and joins the group. "Let me introduce one of my best friends, Jo Barry. This is Andy, Tom and Bucky."

"What a great voice you have, Jo. We really enjoyed the show," says Tom.

"I loved the skit," says Andy, "really cute. I think we should buy these gals a couple of drinks, don't you fellows?"

"They deserve it," adds Tom.

"Then it's settled," says Andy. "We'll just go next door to the bar and celebrate the evening. Is that all right with you both?"

"Great," comes a quick response from Jo.

"I'm really not a drinker. I do wild, passionate things when I drink," I say, jokingly—fearing it might be true.

"Bartender, bring this lady a drink," says Andy.

"We'll meet you over there after we change," says Jo, who then turns to me and asks, "How do you know those guys?"

"I was in a safety class with them. They're all very nice."

"They're going to buy us real drinks, you're not going to order a coke are you? That would look so high school. Promise me you won't order a soft drink. People feel uncomfortable around you when you don't drink with the rest of us. Please order a grown-up drink, for me, okay?"

"Oh, all right. Since it is a special night."

After changing, I make my way through the crowd of familiar faces, accepting compliments and thanks. I enter the bar and find it everything I hate. A huge crowded room, solid with smoke and people over-drinking. But, tonight I'll stay because it's not every day that an astronaut comes into your life. I look around the room and recognize two arms beckoning us from the other side of the room, guarding a small round table like pit bulls.

"Here are the stars of the show," says Tom.

"I don't know about that," I say.

"I found out one thing about you tonight," says Andy. "You have two of the best looking legs I've ever seen."

"I'll bet you've seen quite a few legs in your time, too."

The waitress comes over to take our orders. The guys order scotch, Jo orders a vodka tonic and I say, "I guess I'll have what he's having," pointing to Andy. Big mistake! I turn to Jo and her eyebrows are raised and her head is tilted to one side. I know right away I am out of my element, but I have the mistaken belief that I can handle one or two drinks.

"I can't believe you guys put on that whole show with just employees. How did you ever get rehearsals in and keep up with your schedules?" asks Tom.

"We've been singing together for some time now. We rehearse right after work three times a week."

"That ending was something else. We were all into it…I mean, arms around each other, the swaying, that good ole American spirit. It was great," says Andy.

"You know Martha wrote that skit, too," says Jo.

"It was really cute. Impressive," says Andy.

"Which Apollo mission are you assigned to?" I ask.

"Not sure yet, probably one of the later missions. We've got some backup chores in the future too," says Tom. The waitress comes to the table and places our drinks down.

"This is on me," says Andy as he slaps down a $20 bill. "Especially after you gals gave us such a great show. Let me offer a toast: To Apollo 11, may it be the most perfect launch we've ever had."

"Hear, hear," echoes Tom and Bucky as they bring their glasses to their lips and swallow. I follow with a baby sip of the worst tasting drink in the world.

"I'll add a toast to the team behind our Instrument Unit," says Tom as everyone takes another swig, and I follow.

"I've got one," says Bucky, "…here's to the IBM entertainers."

"I'll have to drink to that, too," I say, as another swig passes my lips.

"Here's to the entire astronaut corps," says Tom.

"Yes, we have to drink to the astronauts," says Jo, as everyone tilts their heads back once again.

"It's my turn," I say. "Here's to President Kennedy for giving us a goal."

"Wonderful," decides Andy.

Jo leans over and tells me, "You're going great. I can't believe you're keeping up with everyone."

Andy turns to Jo and asks, "What do you mean?"

"Everyone knows that Martha can't drink, she's very inexperienced."

Andy turns to me, "Why is that?"

"There's just something about my metabolism that doesn't like alcohol. I always do impetuous things when I drink."

"We'll watch over you tonight and make sure you don't get into any trouble," says Andy.

"Sooo, Andy, do you play any tennis?" I ask, realizing my speech is rather slow.

"As a matter of fact, I do."

"I'll bet she could beat you," says Jo.

"Nah, Andy could beat her in a second," says Bucky. "He beats all of us."

"She's our IBM champion, she beats all the men in our company tournaments," says Jo.

"Wait a minute, Jo. I have to know how good he is at tennis." I turn to Andy and ask, "Have you ever played competitively in high school or college?"

"No. Never on a team."

"Do you play regularly?"

"How could I with my schedule?"

Kevin and his wife come over and join our table. Following introductions, Andy summarizes the situation. "What we have before us is a challenge, the expertise of your company's champion, Martha, against me in a tennis match."

"Oh, she can take you," says Kevin. "I've seen her play. Chris Evert's Dad was her coach."

"All right. If we are to have this match, will we play two out of three sets?" I ask.

"Whatever you say. I really don't know much about how much we should play. I just know I'm a highly competitive guy, athletic, good coordination…that's what I've got going for me."

"Do it Martha. You can beat him," coaxes Jo. "We'll back you up."

"I've got $50 that says she can beat Andy," says Kevin. "It's the IBMers against the astronauts. You guys put your money where your mouth is."

"I'm with our commander," says Tom as he and Bucky search their wallets and bring out $50 between them.

"I'll hold onto the money," says Kevin.

"Martha, it's time to commit. Do we have a match or not?" asks Andy.

I probably wouldn't have taken on the challenge had I been sober but now I can feel the alcohol's warm effect on my body. Being tipsy, I have even more bravado about my skills.

"Okay, it's a match. I'll do it. But, I've had enough to drink, I'm tired and I have to go home now."

Andy, obviously disappointed with my statement says, "Wait a minute, when and where will we play this match? I'm in town until Sunday."

"Okay, tomorrow, Saturday it is. As long as it's in the afternoon, say around 5 o'clock at the Cocoa Beach Tennis Complex." I stand, pick up my purse, and wave goodbye to everyone.

"Let me walk you to your car," says Andy. "You're not going to chicken out are you? You'll probably win, but just to make it more exciting, let's up the ante." As we reach my car, he opens the door and adds, "If I lose, I'll take you to dinner anywhere you'd like...a first class dinner with all the trimmings."

"And if I lose?"

"Then you have to go to bed with me."

"You really are highly competitive...and you're cocky too. You like that sense of danger, don't you? This doesn't change anything. I think I'll still beat you. I play with guys all the time and I beat them," I say, my voice sounding slow and deliberate. "I am flattered that you'd want to include me in the bet. Now, I'm really going to beat you. You need someone to knock you down a couple of notches. You might be a mighty astronaut, with all your astronaut training, but I know tennis," I say as I start the car and put it in gear.

"Okay, I'll see you tomorrow," he says as he closes my car door. "Drive carefully."

Later, as my head hits my pillow and the room spins, I ask myself, did I just make a tennis bet with an astronaut...a tennis match with me in bed as the prize? Nah, it's got to be a dream.

. . . .

CHAPTER 12

THE MATCH

The next morning is a mental washout. The girls have been picked up early by their dad and taken to the airport in Orlando for their flight to Asheville, North Carolina. The way I feel only reinforces the reasons I don't drink—and the number one reason is the day after. My head hurts, my stomach is upset and I, once more, vow never to drink again.

The events surrounding last night's performance seem like a dream, but an exciting dream! Have I really agreed to a tennis match with Andy with my body on the line? I feel I can beat him on most days. With the way I feel right now, though, I'm just not sure that today is one of those days.

What is my fascination with married men? I know there's a fascination with astronauts. We all wonder what they're made of, what drives them. Andy is everything one would imagine an astronaut to be, funny,

A beautiful liftoff! (NASA)

personable and intelligent—and a gentleman. I know I'm trying to find my way since my divorce, just like any other woman.

Maybe spending some time with an astronaut is just want I need to transcend through this breakup with Ed. I certainly don't expect

We entertain at the Quarter Century Club

anything from his friendship. I don't profess to have any real crush on him, only admiration and respect.

I put on some old clothes to paint over the lipstick mural as this will be the only chance I get before the demands of the launch take over my life. I pull my hair back in a ponytail and dip into the paint that is waiting for me in the hall and begin the tedious job. I get no further than one section when the doorbell rings. I put the roller brush down on the paint can lid and head to the door. "Andy, what are you doing here? How did you find my house?"

"I have my ways."

"You're about four hours early."

"I know. I get antsy. I can't stand to be idle. We finished all our practice in the command module early so I thought I'd find you. What are you into?" he asks, as he looks me up and down.

"Let me show you," as I lead him into the hall. "See this beautiful, artistic, mural. It's a creation by my daughters, painted with great love. However, it is made of lipstick and I'm trying to paint over it."

"I understand. Do I hear water running?"

"That's the girls' bathroom. I can't seem to get the toilet to stop running."

"Where's your toolbox?"

"My hands are all messy or I'd get it for you...it's in the garage, on top of the freezer." He disappears and comes back with the toolbox in hand. I can't help but notice he is wearing tennis clothes: blue shorts and a blue and white striped shirt. Not put-together clothes that could pass as tennis clothes, but real tennis clothes. There is a difference and a serious player, like myself, knows it. As he approaches I notice his legs. Perfectly shaped, athletic legs, with nice calves. He has a good build, not overly muscular, his upper torso fits snugly into his tennis shirt and his shorts are filled out completely around his thighs.

He works on the toilet for no more than three to five minutes. "What else do you have that needs to be fixed?"

"There's a window handle above my bed that's frozen."

"I'm on it." I hear a loud sound and the window opening and closing. He returns to me and says, "What else?"

"You do have a lot of energy." I keep painting and try to remember any other items so I can take advantage of this handyman who has materialized at my door. "My TV picture is bad."

"Good, I like to work on TVs."

He disappears again. I hear the TV turn on, then off. Then I hear the song, *My Girl* blaring from the radio as he returns to my side. "I'd hate to pay your hourly rate," I say.

He takes the roller brush out of my hand and lays it across the paint can and whirls me around. "Jeez, someone in my office will ask me 'what did you do over the weekend' and I'll think, Oh, I had an astronaut over to fix my toilet."

"I hope I get to do more than fix your toilet."

"What does that mean?"

"Our tennis match of course. I hope I beat you."

"You're a smooth dancer, too."

"Are you surprised?"

"Not really."

"I thought you'd be a good dancer, and you are."

"I love to dance, I'm a dancing fool." I remind myself that he is married. I've heard about astronaut tales of womanizing around the Cape. Maybe I'm being selfish thinking of my own needs. Maybe I just want to be lifted out of my depression over Ed. Andy takes hold of me and pulls me to him, looking deep into my eyes. He reaches down and plants a sweet, gentle kiss on my lips, a kiss that isn't pushy or passionate.

The music stops and a commercial interrupts the music. "You've done enough work for today. Why don't you change and we'll go play our match?"

"I have this friend who has a house on Merritt Island," says Andy. "He's even got a tennis court. He's given me his keys, as he doesn't even use the house during the summer months. "

"Okay, that's fine with me."

"I'll be just a minute," I say, as I go into my bedroom and close the door. I pull out my favorite tennis dress, the white one with red piping, designed by my friend Mondessa, in Ft. Lauderdale. I put on my tennis shoes and apply my makeup, keeping my hair in the ponytail for our big match.

"That was fast," says Andy as his eyes check out my entire body. "There are those legs. WOW!"

I laugh at his silliness.

"That's a beautiful white cat you've got."

"White cat? What white cat?" I remember the incident with everyone in the family accusing Cindy of imagining a white cat.

"That one over there," he points to a white cat that is calmly walking out onto the back patio through the slightly open sliding glass door.

"Thank goodness."

"What do you mean?"

"It's not our cat. We all thought my daughter was seeing things when she told us about a white cat on her bed at night. I was ready to take her to a shrink," I say as I close the sliding door to the patio and end the white cat mystery forever.

"I'm ready if you are," says Andy. After locking up the house, we get into Andy's red corvette, courtesy of Jim Rathmann's Chevrolet of Melbourne.

"Why don't we stop at Publix and pick up some steaks and we can cook over there tonight?"

"Okay, sounds good."

After picking up steaks, potatoes and salad fixings, Andy picks out a dark red wine to go with the meal. At the checkout counter, no one in the store recognizes him. He doesn't have the life of a movie star, a celebrity that can't venture out of their house without recognition. He certainly looks like everyone else in his tennis clothes.

We drive north on South Patrick Drive, then up South Tropical Trail. Once we leave the narrow road behind, Andy floors it. This man thrives on excitement, and danger. He slows down and turns left into a dirt driveway with a chain and lock on it. He gets out of the car and unlocks the chain…and then relocks after we pass through. After another four hundred yards we reach a beautiful house at the end of the road, a split-level house painted yellow with black shutters and black trim. It sits proudly between two old Florida oak trees covered in Spanish moss.

"My friend found this place and completely redid it from the floor up. It sure has a lot of character, doesn't it?" he says as he turns off the car.

He grabs the groceries and I grab the tennis racquets and balls. "It's gorgeous," I say as we walk toward the door.

"And so private," he adds. He unlocks the door with one hand and opens it for me. "They've really got a special place here. Let me put these down and I'll show you around," he says, putting the groceries on the kitchen counter. "Let's go out back first." He unlocks the sliding doors that lead to the pool area directly behind the house, overlooking the Indian River.

"What a beautiful view…I'll bet the sunsets are pretty special."

"You'll find out the answer to that after dinner. The guy must have three or four lots here because the tennis courts are totally built on their own lot, facing north to south, just the way they should be," he says. We walk through the plush greenery and find a beautiful hard court set in an idyllic spot.

"This court looks brand new," I say. "You're pretty knowledgeable about tennis courts for someone that's not supposed to be very good."

"I just remember what my friend, Mike, told me about his court, that's all."

He takes my hand and guides me to the river's edge and we look across the water to the other side. A breeze slaps the palms of a nearby coconut tree as we walk the length of the boat dock. Hibiscus of every imaginable color blooms profusely, bougainvillea, gardenias and even Birds of Paradise punctuate the lushness of the garden.

"They've got their inboard in storage, but we can use their canoe."

"It's all just magnificent. I feel like I'm in a different country."

"Let's check out the house. It's equally impressive."

"If this is their winter home, I'd love to see their main house. What does this guy do?"

"He's in the oil business. I met him in Houston. He's also got an apartment in New York. He comes down for all the launches, though. He'll have this house filled with friends for every liftoff." As we enter, Andy flicks on the air conditioning and a wave of cool air hits my face.

The living and dining rooms have beautiful hard wood floors with oriental red rugs. The cathedral ceiling is made of fine pecky-cypress wood, stained a light, almost white tone. The couches and chairs are in white and the walls are adorned with original oil paintings and two water colors of blue herons. A long coffee table of travertine marble sits in front of the extra large, U-shaped sofa that can easily seat 15 people.

"He's got three bedrooms, the master is on this side and the guest bedrooms are on the other side," says Andy, pulling my hand along the tour, heading to the master bedroom.

"Wow, that's a huge bed."

"It's a California king," explains Andy. "Mike is 6'6" tall."

The master is decorated in pink and green, with a desk and table sitting by the French doors leading to the patio and pool. The wall-to-wall plush carpeting is a light beige. The bedspread is in a flower print of greens and pinks, with a pink bed skirt. A TV sits on the bedroom dresser.

"Is this bath big enough for you? Look at that huge Jacuzzi, two sinks and a shower." The bath is done in white marble with pink and green towels for accents.

We don't check out the other bedrooms. We head right to the kitchen, Andy chattering all the way about the amenities of this great house. The kitchen has coral tile as a backsplash and white tiles crisscross the floors. The cabinets are a high-gloss white and the counters marble. A commercial refrigerator and freezer sit side-by-side, with wood inserts matching the cabinet wood.

"Do you use this place often?" I ask.

"As a matter of fact, I've never used it before. Only been here for parties. Perfect for our match, wouldn't you say?"

"Yes, indeed. We wouldn't want to play at a large public facility with all we have at stake."

"Can't you just imagine that? If everyone knows what our stakes are, the guys will be rooting for me and the women will boo me every time I make a point."

"I know a lot of women who would like to be in my shoes, win or lose."

"I can tell you right now, there won't be any losers in our match," he says, looking right in my eyes, smiling with his lips closed. "I'm going to grab a beer before we start. Do you want one?"

"No thanks. I've got this important match to play." He disappears into the house and reappears with beer in hand.

"Let's sit over here while I down this baby." We find comfortable sling-back chairs, sit down and relax before the battle of the sexes begins.

"Tell me. How did you wind up as an astronaut?"

"Off the record. To tell you the truth, I have no idea. I just heard the Navy was screening applicants and my name came up. They asked me if I'd like to volunteer and I said, 'Hell yes!' They whittled the group down to about five hundred, then fourteen. The next thing I knew, I was an astronaut."

Just then a jet flies overhead, making a deafening noise.

"Oh, yeah, the only bad thing about this place is we're in the takeoff pattern for Patrick Air Force Base. That's a T-38; it must be one of the crew heading back to Houston."

"Is that what you fly?"

"We all do."

"Do you like everything about your job as an astronaut?"

"None of us like the PR end of it. You know, the hullabaloo of selling the flights. We call it going 'in the barrel.' Then, there's all that time on the road after the flights to publicize it. We're not entertainers or politicians; that part of the mission is foreign and uncomfortable to most of us. Now it's my turn for a question, why did your marriage fail?"

"We got married too young, had children right away. Grew in different directions, wanted different things. I stopped loving him and he stopped loving me. It was a bad match as far as personalities go. I'm outgoing, fun loving, a people person. He's a stay-at-home, never-does-anything type. We're both much happier now. He remarried one month after our divorce. No regrets, though, I have three beautiful, great daughters."

"You seem to be a pretty positive person," he says sipping his beer. "I think it's time for our big match, don't you?"

"I'm ready if you are."

"How long have you been playing tennis?" he asks.

"Since I was about 13. I grew up taking lessons from Chris Evert's Dad, Jimmy." Andy goes over to the broom at the end of the court and begins sweeping the court. It is a beautiful Florida day, the humidity is not so bad, and the sky is blue with very little wind; the perfect day for a memorable tennis match.

The court is in excellent shape, no more than a few years old. The only signs of age are a few mildew spots where a shade tree shields it from direct sunlight. No cracks, or uneven surfaces. The lines are still bright white. A bench sits near the net, about five feet from the court. I put my bag on it and take my sweatbands out, putting one on each wrist. I take my Wilson steel racquet and hit the handle with a bag of rosin. I sit my racquet against the net and start my stretching exercises, leaning against the net. I straddle my legs and stretch one leg at a time. Then I stretch from side to side with my hands on my hips, and legs apart. I twist my body to each side, swinging my arms around my back as far as I can go.

Andy has brought two racquets; he removes the covers and bounces each racquet off the strings of the other, listening for the high pitch that will signal a well-strung, tight racquet. He decides on one and puts the other on the bench.

"I've got balls," I say as I reach into my bag and pull out some Wilsons.

"There aren't too many women who can make that statement. But if any woman does have balls, it would definitely be you," says Andy, with a sly grin. He takes the balls from me and opens the lid to the distinctive sound of the air escaping from the can. This is going to be one hell of a match.

Andy announces the game. "We'll play the best two out of three sets; tiebreaker at 6 all."

"Okay, I'll spin for serve, rough or smooth?"

"I'll take smooth." I put the head of my racquet on the court, spin it and let it fall. I pick up my racquet and show it to Andy. It's smooth. Andy has won the choice.

"I think I'll receive," he says.

"I'll take this side," figuring that the afternoon sun will be in the west shining on the person serving from the east side.

"Good luck," says Andy giving me a wide grin. "May the best man win."

"Good luck yourself. You're going to need it flyboy." We begin hitting from the back of the court first. We exchange forehands for the first five minutes, then backhands. One of my best weapons is my western forehand that I can whip around for sure put-away on short balls. My one-handed backhand is considered by many to be my best shot, especially when I get a target at the net to pass. I can go straight down the line, or cross-court it with amazing speed and strength. After ten minutes, we take the net to hit volleys. My best shot at this range is my backhand volley. I've polished off many an attempted passing shot when my opponent had underestimated my coverage of the alley. My overhead is as good as any man's. It is a crisp, flick of the wrist, with few men in mixed doubles trying to take the shot away from me. I can kill it as well as any man.

"You really hit the ball hard...for a girl," says Andy. "I can see where you'd beat a lot of guys who would try to out-hit you."

I'm quick at the net, too. I can cover a lot of ground and hit that volley back at my opponent's feet. After 15 minutes of hitting, I have analyzed my opponent's game. He has an eastern grip, which means he's taken lessons for some time from a pro. He hits the ball moderately, not hard. I like speed. I like to play off the speed of my opponent. He has a fairly accurate forehand and a pretty good backhand, although I think his backhand is his weakness. He is quick and covers the court well. He's breathing pretty well too; no huffing and puffing on long points, so that means he's in excellent shape, which comes as no surprise.

"You take some at the net," I say as I back up and hit a few right at him. He misses some and gets some. His net play isn't that great, either.

"Ready to take some serves?" I ask.

"Sure, you go first." I take two balls and put one in my tights, next to my skin, on my right side. I serve the first ball to his forehand, the second to his backhand and the third into his body. He returns them all. My serve isn't my forte. It is accurate and I hardly ever double fault.

Andy takes the balls and begins to practice. His serve is fast and powerful, with good control.

"I'm ready when you are," I announce.

"Roger that!" comes his flyboy response. I am ready for battle. I predict that I will win 6-2, 6-2. My game plan is to string him along, make it interesting, let him win a few points, so what? Let him think he has a chance, then come in for the big kill!

"Linesmen ready? Play!" says Andy.

I serve to his forehand and he returns the ball to the middle of the court with little pace on it. I think he's figured out that I like the fastball. Looks like he's going to slow it down. I've seen this kind of tennis before, they loop it, spin it, drop shot it and try to mess up my timing. I wait for his short ball and put it away easily.

After several more minutes of points, all of which I've won, I reassess my role in this match. My job is not to embarrass or humiliate him, or castrate him. Bring him down gently. Make a match of it; make it close.

Andy wins the next two points, which are now lasting longer. I relax. I don't need my A-plus game today. I have no reason to put away every shot so early. There's plenty of time for that later. I win the first game; we change sides and Andy wins the second.

"Good game," I say, projecting my best sportsmanship onto the court.

"I'm just warming up, Tootsie," he says as we change sides and he swats my rear end with his racquet. "Two-one," he announces as an ace flies by me. I try to conceal my shock.

"Good serve," I say, but what I'm really thinking is: What a lucky serve! So he's going to play tough. I take the next serve off my backhand and reel it cross-court for a clear winner.

"You like that fast serve, don't you?" he says.

"I'm not complaining."

On his next serve he hits it slow to my forehand. The shot hits the service line. I try for the cross court, but I hit it into the net. I win the next two games and he evens it up at four-all. We play a tiebreaker at six all. At five-all in the tiebreaker I decide to go for my shots. Andy is still slow-balling me, which makes it hard to get my tempo, plus he's fast, he gets to everything. His sheer determination keeps him in point after point. I'm getting impatient with the slowness of the game. Having difficulty with my rhythm with all the looping shots. Andy hits a drop shot while I am all the way in the back of the court. I get to the ball but over hit it and it goes out.

"I hate drop shots. They ought to be outlawed," I say before thinking. I know never to let my opponent know what bothers me.

"This is set-point," he announces.

"Yeah, yeah. I know."

He serves to my forehand and I let go with a sharp return to his backhand. He loops it back and I run forward to hit my overhead. I'm going to put this baby away as I wind up, point to the ball in the air with my left hand and flick my wrist, sizzling it beyond Andy's reach.

At six-all in the tiebreaker, we change sides. Andy has one more serve coming. If I win this point, I'll be serving for the first set. Andy serves into my body, jamming my return, which I return wide.

"Set point for me," says Andy. It's my serve and I bounce the ball in front of me three times; wind up my serve and let it go.

"Out," yells Andy.

My second serve is half the speed of the first one. Andy wallops it down the line. I get to it and rip it back with a smooth, low backhand cross-court. Andy takes it at the net, hitting to my forehand. My favorite shot is before me: a target at the net and a short shot coming at me. Should I cream him, hit it right at him? That's what I'd do in a tournament. That's the killer shot I'm known for. It's called killer instinct. I've done it a thousand times. This isn't just anyone on the other side of the net. It's Andy: America's hero astronaut. In the seconds it takes for me to wind up, my heart takes control of my racquet and hits a high ball. Andy takes it and puts it away with his overhead.

"First set to Flyboy!" says Andy. He puts his racquet down and waves his hands in the air, up and down.

"What are you doing?"

"I'm trying to quiet down the audience. They're in an uproar. I can't play with all that noise."

I smile to myself. "Good set."

"I hope I didn't make you mad," says Andy. "I can see where you could really be dangerous if you wanted to be."

We begin the second set and I decide that enough is enough. I will play my usual aggressive game. But I am having trouble getting aggressive with Andy. My heart isn't in gear to search and destroy. Andy has me 5-4 when I take the net. I hit a bullet ball and he blocks it back, hitting me in my breast.

"You hit my right breast," I say in disbelief.

"I'm a little off, I was aiming at the left one."

I press my lips together so I won't laugh out loud. I try to concentrate. I shake my head. The truth is I really don't care if I beat him. Why should

I? The stakes are better if I lose. I'm no fool. Just the thought of going to bed with Andy, making love with him, makes me forget all about my tennis form and winning. Let him think he's won me. I was in control of this whole match from the get-go. My, but I've come a long way.

Andy wins the second set 6-4 and I rush the net to congratulate him. I offer my hand, but he kisses me, sweat and all.

"You played well, Andy, you're a fighter."

"That's the best I've ever played in my entire life. But then, I've never had stakes like this before. I was really motivated."

As we head inside, nothing is said about the consequences of my loss as we gather our racquets and place them securely in our tennis bags.

"What'll you have to drink?" asks Andy.

"A coke's fine." He goes directly to the refrigerator and pulls out a beer and a coke. We sit on the couch in the Florida room, off the kitchen, propping our feet on the coffee table before us. A huge TV screen dominates the room surrounded by jalousie windows on three sides and a grass rug on the floor.

"You played well. You deserved to win. You've got a dogged perseverance," I say.

"You never seemed to put your whole game together. You've got a hard-hitting game; I'll give you that. My game plan was to mix it up."

"I did feel out of synch, couldn't get my rhythm going," I say, as all who lose might say.

"No losers, remember. Let's take our drinks and go for a canoe ride. When we get back, we'll clean up and cook our steaks. Sound okay to you?"

"Sounds good. I can't remember the last time I was in a canoe. You probably know all about canoes, too."

"Enough to get us around the river."

With one beer in his hand, Andy picks up another on the way out. I close the sliding doors behind us as we head for the dock. I put my sunglasses back on as Andy flips over the canoe, finding the two paddles underneath.

"Let's leave our tennis shoes here," he suggests. I unlace my shoes, take off my socks and leave them on the dock.

"This canoe is safe, isn't it? We're not going to turn over, are we?"

"Sure, it's safe. You can swim, can't you?"

"No. I can't swim; I'm a tennis player. Don't go near the water."

"You can't swim? I can't believe someone from Florida doesn't know how to swim. How come you can't swim?"

"Just never got around to learning," I say.

"Well, I'll teach you later in the pool. You have to learn to swim."

He holds my hand as I take a step and enter the shaky canoe. He pushes off from the shore and we're on our way. "Here," he says, as he hands me a paddle. "You take the left side and I'll take the right."

"Okay," I answer as I turn around carefully. We start paddling away from shore and in a few minutes we're out in the middle, heading north. We stay out for hours, with Andy eventually telling me to take a rest, as he takes total control over the canoe. He is, in fact, a total control kind of guy. I turn myself around, facing him. Our laughs can be heard echoing across the water. People in other boats pass and wave; we wave back.

"We'd better start heading back," suggests Andy.

"Shouldn't I get back to paddling on my side?"

"Sure, if you want to. Be careful when you stand."

I stand, turn and lose my balance and fall over the side, turning over the canoe and Andy with it. After plunging into the water I kick my feet to propel myself back to the surface in time to see Andy coming at me as fast as he can, with the canoe in tow. It isn't everyday that an astronaut rescues a gal.

He stretches out his arm, grabs me and pulls me towards him. Once I am holding tightly to the canoe he asks, "Are you okay?"

"I'm fine, thanks. I just lost my footing."

"God, it scared me, with you not knowing how to swim."

"Thanks for saving me," I say, looking directly into his eyes as we both hang onto the canoe.

"All I could think was…I haven't collected on our bet yet," he says as a smile creeps across his face.

"You're awful, you know that?" I take my hand and hit the water, splashing it towards him.

"I know, but I wasn't really worried about you. I knew I could get to you. Besides, tomorrow's headlines scared me more… 'Astronaut's friend drowns in Indian River.'"

We both get behind the canoe and push it all the way back to the dock, kicking our feet behind it. Once we reach shore, we collapse on the dock, wet, exhausted, but still laughing.

"That was a good workout," he says, as we catch our breath lying beside one another. "I've got to teach you to swim. Let's jump in the pool while we're still wet and I'll give you your first lesson."

"Great, thank you, master," I say as I stand. My tennis dress isn't meant for swimming and the wetness of the fabric is clinging to my body, revealing my nipples. I see Andy look at me as I run to the pool and jump in the shallow end. He follows me by performing a perfect cannonball, splashing water everywhere.

"First, let me hold you in a floating position on your stomach," he begins as I turn on my stomach and he holds his left arm under me and his right arm on my back. "Now, kick with your legs and move one arm at a time, pulling the water." I follow his instructions, playing my part to the hilt. He glides me around the pool for several minutes, giving more instructions.

"Okay," he says, "Try it on your own." I shove off from the side of the pool and swim the entire length swiftly, with perfect breathing as my head rotates in and out of the water. On the return trip, I change to the backstroke.

"Like this?" I ask.

"You're a devil; and you've been sent to drive me crazy. All this time, and I fell for it. Even in the canoe. What a devil." Andy lunges for me, grabs me and kisses me, this time, very passionately. I can feel his body against mine. I can feel his desire. When he releases me, I lift myself out of the pool and sit by the side, my feet dangling.

"I enjoyed that Andy. I really gotcha there, flyboy!"

"Go ahead, laugh, but know that I will not forget this either. I'd watch out if I were you. I've got a memory like an elephant." He pulls himself out of the pool and sits next to me and announces, "I'm getting hungry. Let's clean up and get our dinner started."

"My problem is I need something else to put on."

"We can stick your dress in the dryer. I'll go in and find something for you to wear," he says as he disappears into the house, returning with several large beach towels and a chenille bathrobe.

"I need you to hold this beach towel up in front of your face and I'll stand on the other side and take my clothes off," I say.

"Why am I doing this?"

"Because I'm too wet to go inside and I don't want anyone in the passing boats to see me." He holds the towel as directed and I slip out of my tennis dress and underwear.

"I can see your underwear at your feet." He says as he takes the big towel and wraps it around me encasing my arms. He kisses my cheeks, then my mouth, and my shoulders.

"Do you want me to hold a towel up for you?"

"Hell, no," he answers as he throws off his shirt, unzips his tennis shorts, removes his underwear, and stands proudly in all his natural glory. I turn to go back in the house, gathering my things, the naked vision still embedded in my thought.

"Chicken!" he yells as he stands stark naked.

"Show-off," I yell back. "I'm taking a shower. I'll see you later," I say, shutting the door behind me. I take a nice shower, find all the right products to wash my hair, put on makeup that's been in my purse and emerge 30 minutes later in the chenille bathrobe. Andy is busy in the kitchen, making a salad, as I smell the charcoal burning and see the steaks waiting at room temperature. He has showered and changed into casual shorts and a Polo shirt.

"Feel better?" he asks as I enter the room.

"I do. How about you?"

"I got some sun today; but I'm not tired. I feel pretty good, in fact."

"How's my dinner coming, even though I don't deserve it."

"You deserve it. Besides I need to feed you to keep your energy level up so you can pay off our bet. I don't want any excuses."

"Get out of here," I say with a smile. "I may have bet my body, but I never said, when."

"Are you trying to renege? I'm going to put the steaks on now. The potatoes have been in the oven for 30 minutes. Grab a beer for me.

Let's go outside and take in that sunset that's been waiting for us." He brings a large platter with two porterhouse steaks piled on top of each other and plops them on the grill. The sun is in the lower part of the western sky reflecting over the river as it begins to set. The golden water carves an area accentuated by egrets flying overhead.

"Beautiful, isn't it," he says as he puts his arm around my waist. "You sure you don't want a beer?"

"No, I'm not a good drinker, you should know that by now."

"Well, it's probably the only thing you're not good at."

"No, I'm not good at balancing my checkbook either."

"Well, you're good at lying; you had me believing you couldn't swim."

"That was a white lie. You deserved it. You beat me and I'll probably never hear the end of it. Besides I've got to break the news to my IBM friends that they lost their money. That's not going to be easy to face," I say as he gets up to check our steaks.

"They seem like a nice, likeable bunch. They'll understand."

"They're a great bunch. We're a very close-knit group."

Andy turns the steaks over and asks, "How do you like yours?"

"Medium is fine," I say and then ask, "How about you?"

"I'm a rare man myself," he replies as he sits back down next to me.

"You seem like you'd be a rare man," I add.

"What makes you say that?"

"The way you live, the excitement, your high energy, your dogged perseverance, your pursuits," I answer honestly. A long pause as we look back over the water, and absorb the beauty of the evening.

"Are you including yourself in my list of pursuits?"

"Am I included?" I have to ask.

"Yes. I'll make no bones about it. I've been attracted to you since the day I met you."

"But, you're married. You have a family. Do you always act on your impulses?"

"If you're asking me if I've had other affairs the answer is yes. But I don't go after everyone that I find attractive," he says honestly.

"How do you do it and still maintain a marriage?" I ask.

"I just happen to believe that we all have to control our own emotions and feelings. I seize the moment and cherish it; but I have other commitments that are dear to me and I honor my promises. Is there anyone else in your life now?" he asks, as he searches for answers in my eyes.

So that's how they do it! The secret is to control our emotions and feelings. Men have been doing it for ages. It's about time that women get with it, too. That's what all the magazines and books on the women's movement are trying to say. Decipher your feelings; don't always attach love to sex. It doesn't work that way. First, find a friend, then let your feelings mature and grow into love, based on mutual respect. Sex is just too overblown. Too many women have married just on the premise of sex when they let their feelings dictate their emotions.

"No, no one in my life right now," I answer his question. "There was a test conductor, but I think I've forgotten all about him."

"I think our steaks are ready," says Andy as he puts the steaks on the plate and we head back to the house where the table is set for two, complete with place mats and matching napkins.

"This is lovely, Andy. Thank you."

"I hope the steaks are as good as they look," he says as he pulls back my chair and we sit down. We unfold our napkins, place them on our laps and head right for the steaks.

"Mine's delicious," I say as I savor each bite.

We eat in silence, enjoying the meal, no one talking for a while until our appetites are satiated. What an awakening I'm having. It puts a whole new light on the subject of love making, sex, affairs, commitments. If we hold onto our feelings and emotions, we're in charge. We're in control. We don't look to another person to bring up joy or happiness. We're complete. It's as simple as that.

"Tell me, what did you think of me that day we met in safety class?" he asks.

I answer, "I thought you had '*the step*.'"

"What does that mean?" asks Andy.

"It's an old southern saying for someone who is confident, intelligent, someone on top of things; a doer, not a taker. Someone you can count on to get things done. One who will take an opportunity and make the most of it," I explain the best I can.

"It sounds like a nice compliment. Thanks," Andy says softly.

"There's always an air of competition with you," I add. "Yes, I was attracted to you but I didn't act on it, knowing you're married. You have free will, you've made a choice, married or not. In the beginning, it was just your astronaut aura, your cockiness, and the way you walk, the way you look in your flight suit. I knew you'd be intelligent, what I didn't know was how charming, how kind, appealing you'd be...and how sexy, too. You have quite a bit of sex appeal."

"That's a nice assessment," he says, smiling.

"You're a special person, Andy, and I'm proud to call you friend," I say with a smile that's been known to melt a heart or two. He puts his fork down and reaches over and kisses me softly on my lips.

"I've suddenly lost my appetite," he says as he stands and takes my hand. "Come on woman, it's time for me to collect." He leads me to Mike's huge bed, throws the cover off and puts both arms around me and kisses me passionately. Oh, he's ready all right. He unties the belt to my bathrobe and it falls to the floor. He pulls off his shirt, pants and underwear in one sweep, faster than an astronaut can maneuver a change of direction.

I want to have sex with him. I am flushed with desire. I want him inside me. I want to experience all there is to this passionate act. He takes his time, surveys the landscape, stakes claim to the prize he's earned. Sure of his procedures he plunges deep into new territory. I believe we have liftoff. The first stage is jettisoned, the second stage separates, the third stage floats away and the spacecraft descends....and we have touchdown!

As the moon shines through the curtains, I remind myself that in a few years Andy will be up there, walking on that same moon. I know I'll remember tonight as I watch him walk on the moon, remembering a tennis match and the sweet spoils that go to the victor. Even if I did lose the match, I gained so much more. How can I know what my needs are except through self-exploration? How can I know who I am and what I value and what will fulfill me without risking intimacy? Can I then, as Andy explains it, control both emotions and feelings in the process? That is the great question.

.

. . . .

CHAPTER 13

AND THEN ALONG CAME JACK

Tennis seems like one of those things that are unessential in life that I can't seem to live without. Good play, competition and winning give me a great high. I've always been grateful for my ability to play sports with no trace of the malady which struck my mother, grateful for my healthy hands and feet.

I'm at a weekend tennis tournament at the Cocoa Beach tennis courts and I've swept the women's singles, doubles and mixed doubles titles. My mixed doubles partner, John Israel, and I are cooling off sitting on a bench waiting for John's new girl friend, Pinky, to join us before he begins his match.

"Good work you guys," says Pinky, referring to our mixed doubles win, as she approaches. "Nice playing."

"Thanks," I say, as she sits beside me to watch John's men's doubles match.

"I've got to get on the court now, " says John, as he picks up his racquet and takes the court right in front of us. Shortly after play begins another gal sits down on the other side of me. She waves vigorously to John on the court. I glance over at her and realize that I don't know her; never seen her before. As I look at her I notice that she and Pinky are wearing the same necklaces. Coincidence? I don't think so. I recall the two necklaces as gifts from our local bank. I remember John recently saying he was also dating someone from Cocoa Beach. Could it be possible that John gave each of them the same necklace? Then, it dawns on me. I've got two gals who are both dating John, one on each side of me. Each staring down the other as much as they can. Whenever John wins a point there erupts massive cheering on either side of me, each trying to outdo the other.

I finally want no part of being in the middle of this threesome. I get up and head inside the pro shop.

"Nice matches out there today," says a guy to my left as I put my money into the coke machine.

"Thanks," I say and turn to look into the dark eyes of a tall, very handsome tennis player dressed in his tennis whites, dark hair, mustache accentuating a dimpled smile, probably around 32 to 34. "Do you play?" I ask to keep the conversation going. I glance quickly at his hand and see no ring on that important third finger.

"Yes, I play regularly out here, mostly doubles."

"My doubles partner and I are always up for some doubles. Would you like to play sometime?" I ask.

"Sure," comes his response. "Do you go with that guy you play doubles with?"

"No, we're just friends. We've been playing tennis together for a long time…but we keep it to the courts." He puts some coins into the machine and another coke shoots out. "Look, I promised John, my doubles partner, that I'd watch his match but I found myself sitting between two girls he's dating, each vying for his attention. It's getting pretty catty out there. I'm going to find another bench, you're welcome to join me."

"Sure," he says and walks with me to a bench outside the pro shop where we sit and continue talking in between the points of the match before us.

"Would you be interested in having dinner with me some time?" he asks.

"I am interested but I live a half hour from here, south, in the Melbourne area."

"No problem, I'll enjoy the ride," he says, as we continue watching John win his match. Following the match we head over to the bench with Pinky and the other gal. John appears to be dumbstruck as to what to do next. As we approach the two women, I overhear the conversation: "John," the other gal yells, "how's your neck?" To which Pinky replies, "His neck was fine this morning when we woke up together."

The other gal, nameless to be sure, is no match for Pinky and stalks off. John, finally feeling safe, joins us and suggests, "Let's go get a pizza and beer somewhere."

I turn to Jack and say, "You're welcome to join us." He does join us. Here is a single man with whom I have tennis in common, who lives in the area, who is also a space worker at the Cape, hired as an electrical engineer for Convair, home to the Atlas vehicle. After chatting through dinner I realize he has a great sense of humor, possibly someone with all the ingredients for a real boyfriend.

At every moment we all have the opportunity to choose the path that will bring us happiness. It is in this choice that love is found. My life is becoming more focused, more able to distinguish between the possibilities of joy or despair. How much more delightful to have someone's interest on a regular basis with the ability to ripen to fruition. A few months ago, I wouldn't have had the courage to speak first to invite him to join us. I'm confident now, at ease with others and myself. I am at a point where I can choose love, not fear or suffering at the mercy of another's rejection, not set myself up for heartbreak. I now feel like I am taking responsibility for my thoughts, actions, feelings and behavior.

I know one thing. I don't love Andy. I admire him and adore him but I'm not in love with him. It's been a learning experience that I've cherished and enjoyed. I am now giving myself the possibility to fall in love, to put before me all the ingredients that have the ability to blossom and grow into love.

The next time Andy is in town, he calls me immediately as soon as he lands. "Hi, how are you IBM?" he begins.

"I'm doing just great, thanks."

"Are you up for dinner tonight?"

"No, I can't make it anymore Andy. I've met someone. I'm going to move on. I've really enjoyed my time with you."

"Thank you," he says. "He's going to be one lucky guy."

"You're going to get so busy with your training. Before you know it you'll be stepping on the moon to take your place in history. It will be just awesome. My prayers and thoughts will be with you."

"I wish you nothing but the best," he says.

After we hang up I realize there are no tears, no regrets, no harsh words, only gratitude for the many lessons learned. I look forward to the months ahead to see just what will unfold now that I've taken this positive step.

There are two parties that rock following the launches; one is hosted by IBMer Nino Perez, who heads our art department, the other is the party given by Lee and Arlene Caron, local entertainers and owners of a bar on the beach.

I'm not really a party girl since I don't drink and that essentially is the prevailing theme that rallies the work force to unwind at both of these parties. Curious, I decide to go with Joanne to see exactly what takes place, planning to attend both parties tonight.

I follow Joanne as she's attended both parties and knows the way. We drive separate cars, first to the Cocoa Beach house located on one of the canals. We find parking several blocks from the Caron's home. As we walk toward the house, the music vibrates and directs us at least a block before we get there.

"It's a magnificent house," says Joanne, dressed in slacks and a tight top, revealing her generous breasts. "The Carons are real chummy with politicians and the astronauts."

I'm dressed in white bell-bottom pants, and a red and white polyester top, my long hair put up in a Gibson. The house is huge; a large swimming pool is centered around the Florida patio, with wings of the house on either side. Waiters run through the house, filling drink orders for whatever guests may want from the endless, well-stocked bar. A band plays from the opposite end of the pool area. The party must have been underway for hours since the house is wall-to-wall people already. I recognize several state senators and congressmen and a few astronauts standing around, drinks in their hands. I speak to Eddie Harrison from NASA public affairs, as well as the PR guy from GE. I don't see anyone from IBM.

We order our drinks, a coke for me, and a gin and tonic for Joanne.

"How's it going with you and Tom," I ask.

"Really good," says Joanne. "He should be arriving soon."

Joanne met Tom, the other writer in our department, when she was working at the VAB. He interviewed her for an article he was writing for our in-house publication for National Secretary's Day. Joanne, a talented, sharp gal, also had to begin as a secretary. Later, she moved to the communications department to help out as a writer. We both have come up through the ranks.

Tom needed a partner for the IBM bowling league and Joanne volunteered. She was immediately attracted to him, even though he is ten inches shorter than her. The height difference didn't seem to bother Tom either, although in the beginning he didn't seem interested in an exclusive relationship. Later, they became inseparable.

Joanne has one of those big laughs, the kind that makes you laugh too. She laughs at all of Tom's jokes and witty sayings. He keeps us all in stitches but has captured Joanne as his number one fan. Nothing is off limits for his humor. He cuts down Warren, himself, Joanne, anyone, but in the most kind way, nothing offensive. He just has this knack to weave some humor into every subject. He is entertaining, usually the life of the party.

"In fact, we're getting married soon," says Joanne. "I didn't want to say anything until after I mail out the invitations."

"That's wonderful. I had no idea you guys were that close to making it permanent," I say louder, as I have to raise my voice over the noise.

After about 30 minutes Tom joins us dressed in a leisure suit, he grabs his drink and settles by our side.

"Congratulations, Tom. I just heard the good news," I say.

"Thanks, I thought I'd get her off my back and make an 'honest woman' out of her," he says with a chuckle.

There is no place to sit. Some are dancing, well, moving their bodies as much as they can. After the attractive blond next to Tom throws up, we jump away, holding our noses. I can't remember who suggested it, Joanne or Tom, but it wasn't me, someone says, "Let's go to Nino's. I don't know anyone here. It's so crowded we can't even talk. Free drinks aren't worth this."

Forty-five minutes was all the time we spent at the Caron's party. In fact, I never even met the host and hostess. As we walk to our cars, we pass someone who has passed out in the backseat of a convertible. Upon closer look, I recognize the guy as a member of our first group of astronauts.

"Hard day at work, commander?" asks Tom who also recognizes one of our heroes.

"You know what? With all those guys go through, the pressures and schedules, if he's found a way to unwind and forget about work," I say, "it's none of our business."

"The astronauts aren't perfect for heavens sake. God bless him," says Joanne adding to our rationalization of the astronaut's actions.

We reach Nino's house in Cocoa in about 20 minutes, obvious that a party's going on but not quite as loud or crowded as the Caron's house.

Nino Perez is a Puerto Rican who transferred from the Owego IBM facility. He is in his late forties, medium height, dark build, black hair and wide set eyes. Another constant smoker, he is a partier of the highest magnitude. His launch parties, which also feature heavy drinking and late hours, are famous. NASA employees, the astronauts, the contractors, the entertainers, and the politicians also show up at Nino's.

He's a likeable guy who would do anything for his friends. You don't simply show up for Nino's parties, like the Caron's. You either respond to an invitation from Nino, or you come with someone who is invited. Of course, anyone who works for IBM is welcome. Just as NASA's Manned Flight Awareness reception is the most coveted invitation for the night before launch, Nino's parties are the place to be following launch. No matter how many hours one has worked through launch, if you can still walk and have an invitation, you make it to Nino's.

The house is much more modest than the Caron's. It's a concrete block, three-bedroom house, with mix-matched furnishings as well. A small pool is in the back of the house. But it is the warmth and fun, the camaraderie that pervades that attracts everyone.

As soon as we walk in, Kevin Griggs sees us and heads directly to me.

"Boy, I really got back at old Waldo last weekend," says Kevin.

"What did you do now?" I ask.

"I ran over to his house while his garage door was open and copied his electric garage door combination. Then I went to Sears, bought an extra clicker and programmed in his combination. I sit at my window, watching TV and him. Every time he closes his garage door, I open it. He'll close it again, walk inside, and I'll click it again. He'll run out, trying to find out what's happening. Now I can just sit back, watch a little TV, aim the clicker over and get him going any time of the day or night. It's driving him crazy."

"Poor Waldo," I say.

"He's not poor Waldo. The guy's a jerk. His yard is a mess, his dog barks all the time, he doesn't discipline his kids and he beats his wife."

"I know one thing," I say, "he should never mess with a creative space engineer!"

I speak to all my friends, thank Nino and Terry, and head home after 45 minutes. It's late and I've got another 60 minutes for my drive home. I decide that's enough partying for this gal.

CHAPTER 14

. . . .

COUNTDOWN DEMONSTRATION
TEST / THE GERMANS ARRIVE

There are no costumes and no makeup, but it is a dress rehearsal that has the whole world as its audience. The stage is the firing room, jammed to capacity with launch team leaders, dressed in their logo jackets, adorned with their headsets. Early this morning the launch crews begin the Countdown Demonstration Test, or CDDT, the final major test for Apollo 11. The test will determine readiness and give a green light to launch America's first men to land on the moon.

CDDT will run for ten days, concluding on July 3. It will include all the steps of the actual countdown, all the tests, a complete fueling of the vehicle, as well as the astronauts in place inside the spacecraft. During this time, only personnel critical to the test are permitted in the firing room. Others, like me, and the entire administrative support team back at the Cape Canaveral building, await word of progress on the test.

Dressed in my miniskirt, an industrial scale provides my accurate weight

We make it to the moon! (NASA)

As Ellie, Tom, Joanne, Bob and Clark, two of the three technical writers, gather in Warren's office for a meeting, he gives us the most up-to-date account.

"CDDT is going well. There have been no problems and we're on schedule."

"Great," says Joanne as we all let out a sigh of relief.

"I don't envy those guys out at the Cape one bit. They're on a 12 on, 12 off schedule—work 12 hours, off 12 hours. Just like launch-time," says Tom.

"Getting back to schedules, let's talk about launch assignments, as well as story ideas. IBM has leased three boats to accommodate the VIPs we expect. Those boats will depart from Cape Canaveral and view the launch from the Banana River. Refreshments will be served; we'll have radios on board. Joanne, you cover one of the boats."

"Got it. Those boats will offer a great view," says Joanne.

"Tom, you go with the bus group to the Holiday Inn in Titusville, where we've made plans to secure their parking lot for one other group. The bus will depart from the back of our building."

"Got it. Should I take my camera, too?"

"Yes, all of you take cameras. Martha, you'll be at the Press Site. The bus taking you there will also depart from the back of our building."

"Okay," I say, happy with my assignment with the top VIPs who will be assigned the press box, which is also the closest to the pad, a mere three miles.

"Ellie, you cover the Manned Flight Awareness reception the night before the launch and be on one of the boats." My heart sinks. I know Andy will be at that reception and I had hoped to garner that assignment. The MFA reception before Apollo 11 will honor workers who have reached a level four of NASA's awareness program. Many are nominated for outstanding work but a level four indicates a person who has achieved such a high level of awareness that his actions probably saved a mission, or a life. It is the ultimate honor for any member of the Apollo team.

"I'll be in the IBM control center here in this building. We'll have three television sets, radio and the NASA drop line. The control center will be the focal point for all information on the status of the launch vehicle, spacecraft and sequence of events. In the event of an emergency which impacts the launch schedule, or involves IBM personnel, or the company's reputation, the incident will be passed on to key designated personnel.

"We'll also maintain a list of all visitors and Cape Kennedy Facility employees involved in the launch. The list will specify launch locations, telephone numbers, as well as the telephone number of all our visiting executives and their motel accommodations.

"The facility control center will be manned from T-28 hours until T-plus seven hours. Only authorized people will be allowed in the center. We'll have technical people in the backup firing room to explain any anomalies to us, so we can then put out the correct news information. We'll also have communications people standing by at our other IBM locations, including Owego, Huntsville, Gaithersburg, and Armonk. We'll have a pressroom set up in Houston, too.

"We're expecting 3,000 journalists to attend this launch and most of them are foreign. The contractors will set up a press center at the Quality Motel. You'll each be required to man the center and help out in any way you can. We'll have hundreds of telephones available for the press to call in their stories. Every TV network is coming, not only from America but also from all over the world. We've even got an Australian marathon runner who's jogging all the way from Houston. And Reverend Ralph Abernathy will be protesting the cost of the program in lieu of the needs of the poor people of the country. We've got it all," concludes Warren.

Warren's phone rings and he stops the meeting to take the call, which must be important, or his secretary wouldn't have put it through. While he's talking I lean over to Ellie and ask, "How set are you on covering the MFA reception?"

"I've covered them before. It's a madhouse, wall to wall people," she says.

"Would you like to trade your assignment with me? I'll give you the press site for the MFA reception and the boat assignment."

"Sure, that's fine with me, as long as Warren goes along with it."

A wide grin flashes across Warren's face. "I just found out that Thomas Watson, Jr. is definitely going to attend launch."

A hush falls over our group. It is as if he said, "Jesus is coming to the launch." There isn't an IBMer alive who doesn't know the story of Thomas J. Watson, Sr. and his son, Thomas J. Watson, Jr., who for sixty years built the international colossus that is IBM. It is their management insights, their integrity and foresight that has, and is, shaping IBM's course and its unique corporate culture. It was Watson, Sr.'s charismatic style that made him one of America's most beloved bosses. It is the daring decisions by Watson, Jr. that are spearheading the transformation of IBM into the world's largest computing company.

"He's bringing Robert Montgomery, the movie star, along with his son and daughter. There will be a luncheon for the entire facility immediately after the launch and Watson will address our entire team," says Warren. "He's even going out to the VAB to personally meet with some of the IBMers out there."

"Wow," says Tom. "I just might have to get a haircut."

With Warren in such a good mood, I lean over to him and ask, "Would you mind terribly if Ellie and I switch assignments? She really doesn't care to cover the reception and gets seasick so I've offered to trade the press site and do one of the boats, if that's okay with you."

"Is that right Ellie?" he asks.

Ellie's deep in another conversation and assumes that I have just asked Warren for the change in assignments. "Oh yes, that's okay with me." Warren takes his pen in hand and changes the lineup for assignments.

"Bob, I'd like you to do the story on launch readiness for outside release," continues Warren.

"Martha, prepare something on our space veterans for *THINK MAGAZINE*. You know what I'm talking about, the guys who have been around here since Mercury and Gemini. Let's get their impressions, their current duties, what they foresee for the future."

"Got it," I answer.

"Joanne, how about something on launch preparations, the control center, how we're handling the visitors...the display that is going on in the cafeteria on IBM's history in the space program," instructs Warren.

Thinking ahead to my own daily and weekly in-house papers, I ask, "Can we print a photo of Watson attending the launch or thanking the launch team?"

"Only in the in-house publications. He wants to be low-key, in the background. He feels it's our show and wants to keep it that way. Let's see ...we'll also print a timeline activities chart depicting vehicle, spacecraft and crew activities from liftoff through the entire mission. That should be enclosed in the VIP's package of goodies too. Martha, you can get that from our communications plan."

"I've got it on my desk," I reply.

"Well, that's all I've got. Don't forget your activity reports are due Monday. There's one more important item," he says as he turns to Jo. "Please bring him in now."

We all watch the door as a fiftyish heavy-set man, with gray hair enters.

"I'd like to introduce the newest member of our department, Cecil Stoughton. Cecil was formerly with the Army, assigned to the White House; in fact, he became Kennedy's photographer. He's also the one who snapped those official photos of the swearing in of Lyndon Johnson aboard Air Force One," says Warren as Cecil shakes everyone's hands, and we introduce ourselves.

I remember the photo not so much for the swearing in, but for the bloodstained dress that Jackie Kennedy wore in the picture. It was a horrible day for all of us and I can only imagine how bad it was for Cecil.

"Cecil isn't coming aboard just yet but will be helping us a little later. He's retiring to Florida and just wants to keep active. So we'll look forward to him joining us in a couple of months," explains Warren. Cecil sits down in the only available chair in the room.

The next morning I head to the Cape for my veteran's interview with Clancy Boswell at exactly 10 a.m. At that time, Clancy will leave his position in the firing room, where he manages the Saturn Support Programming group, to break away from the test at that particular time because the vehicle will be undergoing fueling operations. I go toward his office on the sixth floor of the VAB high bay. This means I will have to transgress the famous catwalk where all the whistles and hollering goes on. As I approach the catwalk I decide I can experience it either as a big insult or just play along with it. I decide not to take offense but to go along with it. As I take my first steps, the whistles begin, then the yells, the choice words that can only describe a woman in the eyes of these men: "Hey baby, you got just want I want!" "Look at those legs and that butt!" "I like her boobs…gimme those tits!" I hurry my pace, until I reach the middle of the catwalk, I take my right arm and put it up high and wave to them, just as if I'm the Queen of England, with the royalty wave. I am not going to let them embarrass or humiliate me. I am standing up to them; not like so many other women who flee in tears, not me, as I clinch my jaw and find Clancy's office.

Clancy has the one thing that Nelson looked for when he recruited the original 15 IBMers who've been invited to kick off IBM's emergence into the space program. He is a field engineer with aerospace experience, a commodity uncommon among the IBM ranks at that time.

"How did it all begin for you, Clancy?" I ask. He begins to tell me his story. "I was at Patterson field and received a call from this guy named Nelson. He introduced himself. Well, I had never heard of him so I ask him, 'Who the hell are you?'

"'I'm your manager's boss, that's who I am,' he says. I didn't care who he was even then. Said he wanted to talk with me at dinner that night. I met him for dinner at Sutt Miller's Supper Club in Dayton. We had drinks, ordered dinner and then he began to explain that IBM was trying to penetrate the space business and asked me to join the team. As he told it, I'd first go to Huntsville for two months of training to learn guidance and control functions, then on to Cape Canaveral.

"I asked him in my usually blunt way, what the hell's in Huntsville or Cape Canaveral? He came back to me with a stinger, saying, 'Well, do you want to go to Goddamn Huntsville and Goddamn Cape Canaveral and work on the space program, or do you want to go to Goddamn Owego and build relays?'

"I reply, I guess Huntsville and the Cape sound pretty good.

"He told me to take two weeks vacation, and if we got the contract I'd go to Huntsville. I got a call from my manager saying we'd lost the contract and to head to Owego. Then two days later I got another call, saying NASA had reversed its decision and we'd won the contract, so I headed for Huntsville."

Once at the Cape, Clancy excels and moves up the Cape ladder. He quickly earns a reputation as a hard worker, a knowledgeable engineer and sensitive manager. He's a happy go-lucky, no-nonsense kind of a guy, who smiles most of the time; a guy that everyone immediately likes. At 6 feet even, black hair and dancing brown eyes, he's as charming as any guy can get.

It's after the Apollo 1 disaster that Clancy and his group move over to the Saturn V side of the Cape to the huge VAB and begin preparing for manned flights to the moon.

"Clancy," I say, "I'm interested in some of your reflections on what Apollo 11 means to you. You're one of the original 15 IBMers who've been here since the beginning. In just a few days, we'll launch three guys to the moon. What are your thoughts?"

"Today, I'm concerned with the tests we're running. We don't have the opportunity to post test a vehicle. It goes once and that's it. We have to be very exact in our testing. Three years ago, the likelihood of a manned lunar landing by 1970 seemed pretty remote. I was working on the program, but it was hard to relate my work to the goal. Now, seeing the fantastic strides we've made, the association is clear and strong. The landing will be a wonderful climax. To tell you the truth, I had my doubts. But, as I've worked on the program and seen the outcomes of Apollo 9 and 10, I'm a believer."

His phone rings loudly beside us. "Excuse me, but my secretary's out sick. Clancy Boswell," he says into the phone. He pauses, shakes his head.

"Ken, don't worry. I'll look into it. Just be cool." He hangs up and explains, "Seems we've got a slight personality conflict with our guys and the NASA LV-CAP-A. Oh, that's the Launch Vehicle Communications and Programming guy. But that's nothing new. I'll iron it out."

"How's the test going?"

"The test is going great. It's all the other human problems I've got to handle in addition to the technical side. I've got one guy who we're trying to get deferred from the draft. That's a day-by-day thing. Another guy's wife is expecting a baby in a month and she's been hospitalized. He's as nervous as hell about losing their baby. I got all kinds of people upset with all the overtime we're working. One guy doesn't want to work the second or third shifts at all. I've got three shifts going all the time for this test and probably through launch. Then, there's another fellow with a broken down car and no transportation to get out here. Another one with four speeding tickets; one more and he'll lose his license. And…a secretary that's sure sick a lot. This place is a zoo!"

The phone rings again. "This is Clancy. Hi, Stella." He listens for a while and then begins: "Okay, let me get this straight, IBM Huntsville is sending down seven guys for the launch and they all expect to sit in the alternate firing room? Well, I can tell you right now, you can send as many guys down as you want, but only two guys from Huntsville are going to be allowed in the alternate firing room. The others can sit in the office. Tell him I said that. Only two."

"I can see you never have a dull moment out here, that's for sure," I say.

"We have our challenges," says Clancy. "Yesterday, Nelson brought out some corporate guys and they noticed Ken's hardhat had more than the IBM logo attached to it. My guys like to put humorous sayings on their hats. What the hell? It's his hardhat. Besides that, the guy's a genius. Nelson told me that he really shouldn't have all those sayings on his hardhat. I took one look at Nelson and said, 'Ken is competent, so we let him keep 'em.'"

"What's this I hear about Nelson pulling some sign down?" I ask.

"You know how everything out here has a label on it? You can't move without reading a label. Even the door has a label that reads STAIR. One of our guys stuck up a sign over it that reads. '*This is not a stair, it's a door.*' Of course Nelson didn't see the humor in that at all. He ripped it off."

"You don't seem to be intimidated by Nelson like some of the others."

"Nah, I just concentrate on doing my job. The other day I had to go down to his staff meeting. He told me to be there at 8 sharp. It was for a 'human error' meeting."

"What's that?" I ask. "I've never heard of that kind of meeting."

"Anytime we've had any kind of an error that was caused by a human, by one of our employees, the person who committed the error, his immediate manager and the next level manager, has to appear before Nelson's staff and explain what happened. We also have to tell what steps we've taken to ensure that it will never happen again. Well, it was an extremely busy day at the VAB with major tests running. We got there shortly before 8 and for one-half hour we sat outside the conference center listening to Nelson rant and rave inside. He was 'eating all their lunches.' Finally, at 8:30, I banged on the door. Nelson came to the door. He had his jacket off and his sleeves rolled up. He was really tearing into somebody.

"I said, what the hell's going on in there? We've been waiting for one half hour out here. Nelson whispered quietly to us that we could all leave. He shut the door and started yelling again."

"You've got a special relationship with him, Clancy. He really respects you. You can get away with things that others would never even attempt."

The phone rings again and Clancy answers it. "Hi, Mike. Yes, Ken's going to teach a class on that. He'll instruct all the Guidance and Computer people on the care and feeding of the OOPSYS. That's going to be held two weeks from today. I'll put you down."

I start to speak but the phone rings once more. "Hi, Tom," says Clancy. "We decided if the function executor problem is encountered again and causes a recycle, the patch will be installed; otherwise, it will not be used." He pauses and concludes, "Okay, good."

"I've got plenty I can use here," I say. "I'll get the draft to you for your approval within the next few days. I really appreciate your time. Hope your secretary gets better," I say as I rise to head back to my office.

I arrive early to go over preparations for Nelson's speech to a group of German VIP's later today. He'll be taking them to KSC for rollout and returning for a catered lunch in the conference room. A specific request was made from the group for a talk on the benefits of space, which I have researched and will have in final form, complete with slides, when the group arrives.

As I double-check the carousel of slides to the corresponding numbers in the triple-spaced script, my eyes catch my in-basket and find about

15 Speak Up! envelopes waiting to be opened. Speak Up!s are of tremendous importance; not only does top management get involved but so does division and corporate. The red complaint and comment envelopes can get attention faster than anything. I open the first one and read: "I resent Mr. Nelson yelling at those of us who were late on Monday. I worked all weekend. In fact, I worked a total of 82 hours that week, without extra compensation."

I open another and read: "Nelson is way out of line with the way he handles tardiness. I was humiliated and embarrassed. I have never missed one day of work here since I began in 1965. I didn't deserve this."

I open another: "Corporate should take a closer look at Nelson's antics. His 'late' confrontation with employees is another example of his dictatorship. We are so far removed from corporate or division that he thinks he can get away with murder. Well this time he has gone too far."

One more reads: "I've only been late a few times in my entire life. I called my manager to let him know I had a sick child and would be coming in late. He gave me permission to take my daughter to the doctor. I almost cried when Mr. Nelson stopped us at the back door."

And another, "I don't even work at the building in Cape Canaveral. I work for RF Systems at the VAB. I had already reported to work at 0600 and left to attend a meeting there. Our holy facility manager called me on the carpet for being late. Not only did he read us the riot act but also he wouldn't even let us explain."

About half the employees who were tagged for being late by Nelson wrote Speak Up!s. The others, like my manager, Warren, had no excuses. I recognize the fact that these are 'hot' Speak Up!s. I immediately type up and log the complaints and head to the director of Personnel, Bob Jones, to let him know what has transpired.

"Is he in?" I ask of Kay Thompson, his secretary. Kay is one of those smiley, bubbly people who always appear to be 'up.' I know differently because I've been her sounding board for her husband's drinking problems. She is in her forties, looks young, has blond hair and a few freckles. She and her husband Brad have one son.

"He's on the phone, but shouldn't be long if you care to wait."

"I'll wait. I've got some Speak Up!s he needs to see. How are things going with you?"

"Brad went for counseling at the Brevard Mental Health Center and he's attended his first AA meeting this past weekend. I have hope because he's finally admitted that he has a problem."

Brad is an engineer with North American, part of the team that supplies the second stage of the Saturn V. Brad was also around when the hammer came down for the Apollo disaster, putting some of the blame on lack of planning, or late or incomplete engineering. Kay thinks her husband took it personally and tries to drown it with a bottle.

"Counseling and AA...that's great news and a step in the right direction." The light on the telephone console goes off, indicating the end of the phone conversation. "You can go in Martha," says Kay.

"There are 14 Speak Up!s in this folder, all on the same topic...the most I've ever received...all about Nelson pulling them over when they arrived a few minutes late," I say to Bob Jones as his eyes light up with the very mention of so many SU's.

"I heard about it, but I didn't know he was going to do it ahead of time. He certainly didn't consult me," says Bob, a fiftyish, balding guy, with an overly round middle. I respect him because he is fair, even-tempered and treats everyone with great respect…exactly what his job description calls for. He has been the soothing rod for Nelson's explosive temper, often calming those upon whom Nelson has unleashed his fury. One of his main jobs is to clean up situations exactly like this one.

After reading my typed list of the SU's, he says, "All these writers are justified. C'mon, let's go see Nelson." With the folder in hand, he bounds up from his chair and leads the way down the hall.

Jo greets us as we enter Nelson's outer office and Bob says calmly, "We need a few minutes of his undivided attention on a very important subject."

"He does have a few minutes before he leaves for the VAB with the Germans; go right in." As we enter, Nelson gives us a big, friendly smile. His office is large but Spartan. An over-sized mahogany desk, launch pictures, a Saturn V model, a couch, and a round table with four chairs complete the room. The only window in the room oversees the driveway into the company parking lot. Nelson is behind his desk, granny glasses atop the bridge of his nose. I feel that Nelson respects Jones and relishes his advice on any personnel question.

"Martha has just brought in 14 Speak Up!s, the most we've ever received on one subject at this facility. They're all complaints about your actions yesterday regarding late employees." He hands the folder to Nelson and he begins to read silently as we take our seats. He slowly shakes his head, puts the paperwork down, elbows resting on his desk, folds his hands together over his mouth and says, "They're right, of course. I only wanted to get the habitual people. It was one of those spur-of-the-moment things when I called someone and they weren't in yet. I felt right about it at the time—justified. I had been studying a Bart chart and realized how little time is left, and how much we have to accomplish. I panicked," he pauses. "I regret my actions."

It is vintage Nelson, dramatically revealing his soft side. A side he only allows a few people to see.

"I know your first concern is for the success of the mission. I also know you care about these people. Most of them would walk through fire for you," says Jones.

"I guess the tension, the fear of failure, the enormous responsibility is getting to me. Have we done enough? Have I pushed hard enough? Is there anything I'm forgetting?"

"You have every right to be concerned. That's your job, but you can't take it out on the people. You have enough to worry about without addressing tardiness. It's really each manager's task to address the subject in his own way," says Jones in a nice smooth tone, never raising his voice to a higher level.

"And I know that!" snaps Nelson. "It just hit me when I was sitting here at my desk and saw all these cars rolling past my window late. I just didn't think they understood the urgency of every second."

"No one has worked harder than you, John. You never expect anything from anyone that you wouldn't do yourself. Let me assure you that our employees do know the urgency of the moment. We've got a great bunch of highly dedicated people who are giving 110 percent already. There's a sense of deep pride among them, and dedication. We don't want to belittle them; we want to be grateful for them. I know Corporate is going to be all over us on this after Martha calls them and lets them know the subject matter.

"Martha," continues Jones, "You go back and write the answer so you'll have it in place when they call. And they will call."

"I know the first rule in answering an SU is to take responsibility when you're wrong…and I was wrong," says Nelson.

"I'll get to it right away," I say and then turn to Nelson and add, "I'll be working the slide projector for your speech to the Germans. What time do you want me there?"

"Why don't you join the group for our tour and then lunch. I'm sure the Germans will enjoy having an American woman in the group. We'll be back for lunch at noon."

I return to my office and immediately begin to draft the answer to the Speak Up!s.

Dear IBMer:

You're absolutely right. I did go too far in addressing tardiness. In trying to make my point as to just how crucial every second is during this time, I forgot about respect for the individual. I forgot that there are no black and white incidents. We all, on occasion, have legitimate reasons for being late. You did have a valid reason but there are those who have fallen into a routine of tardiness. It was to those individuals that my actions were directed. I felt their actions were demoralizing to those who do their jobs and arrive on time. I assure you this will never happen again.

Please accept my apology. I greatly appreciate your efforts, your dedication and your understanding in this matter.

Thank you for expressing your feelings on this subject.

J. L. Nelson

I grab my purse and head out back to join one of the three cars transporting the Germans to the crawlerway. Nelson purposely parks the caravan one-half mile from the VAB. The massive doors of the VAB bays are still shut.

I know the sequence very well. Rollout occurs after the electrical systems of the rocket boosters are mated with those of the spacecraft. Crane operators do the actual stacking 462 feet above the VAB floor. They use digital computers and listen over earphones to the men who stand beside each segment to detect movements and tolerances of as little as 1/128th of an inch. If vertical balance is lost, the whole thing could fall over and become a billion-dollar pile of junk.

Nelson begins to speak, holding them spellbound as they try to comprehend the complex performance unfolding before them. "The six million-pound transporter travels on four double-tracked crawlers the three and one-half miles to Pad 39A. Each of the crawler shoes," he says, "weighs one ton."

"Where did they come up with this design?" asks one of the Germans.

"I believe it was modeled after the steam-shovel tractors used in the open-pit coal mines of Kentucky. This crawler is as big as a baseball diamond," says Nelson.

"It's opening," yells someone in our crowd. One of the black doors of the VAB bay starts opening upward. Slowly and precisely, the doors reveal the masterpiece it has been protecting, the treasure its people have created and worship. First in view, from the bottom, are the giant "shoes" of the transporter. Atop the transporter is the mobile launcher with its two-story steel structure at the base. As the doors open completely, the whole vehicle stands proudly, hugged by nine swing arms.

"It's majestic!" says one of the Germans. "But, tell me why don't you just assemble it all at the pad?"

"We used to do just that," says Nelson. "From 1958 until just a few years ago, the fixed launch concept was used in all NASA missions. We assembled, checked it out and launched from one site. But NASA found it tied up the launch pad and it left flight equipment exposed to corrosion, storms and hurricanes.

"Having the vehicle thoroughly checked in the VAB before it is moved to the pad for finals affords greater protection from the weather, more systematic checkouts and higher launch rates. Pad time is minimal," Nelson says.

The stacked bird makes its first forward movement, edging out from the VAB. The crowd applauds as if a leading lady has stepped on stage for her curtain call.

"This is a great thing, a wonderful sight, an honor to see this happening," another guest says.

Nelson speaks again. "It takes an 11-man crew onboard and a 3-man ground crew to operate this baby. You'll see that there are two operator cabs, one at each end of the chassis. It will take almost eight hours with a maximum speed of one mile per hour to reach its final resting spot on the pad. The top of the space vehicle is kept vertical within plus-or-minus 10 minutes of arc. This system will keep the vehicle level when it goes up the five-degree ramp leading to the pad.

"The cost of this road, this crawlerway we're standing on was $7.5 million. It's topped and sealed with asphalt, then covered with eight inches of river rock to reduce friction," concludes Nelson.

We all get back in the cars, and park closer to the VAB. We get out and walk through a limited area of the transfer aisle and view one of the firing rooms. We arrive back at the Cape Canaveral building on schedule at 11:45, giving everyone time for a break before lunch and Nelson's speech.

During lunch one particular German comes over to me and says, "Are you available for dinner tonight?"

"No, sorry, I'm not. Thank you anyway," I say, being careful not to offend our guest.

"You know I am quite wealthy. I am president of my company. I have a plane at my disposal. Will you reconsider?"

I wonder if all Germans come on this strong. "Sorry, I can't make it," I say, smiling.

"I will make it worth your while," he continues.

"I have to go to work now," I say as I head to my position at the back of the room where the controls to the slide projector are located. Nelson pushes a button and the curtains separate, revealing the screen.

Nelson starts, "Gentlemen, I trust everyone has been sufficiently nourished. Please sit back, relax and enjoy your coffee while I attempt to answer the questions you requested of me before your visit. You asked me to tell you 'why America is exploring space.'

"I'll begin with a quote from one of America's most esteemed senators: *'What do we want of the vast worthless area? This region of deserts, of shifting sands, and whirlwinds of dust? To what use could we ever hope to put these deserts or these endless mountain ranges? What use can we have for such a place? I will never vote one cent from the public treasury.'*

"Gentlemen, this senator who gave this speech was not referring to the moon, but to California. More than 125 years ago, Daniel Webster opposed the appropriation of $50,000 for mail service to the west.

"It will cost us $24 billion for Apollo. That comes to $120 for every American citizen over a nine year period. But, you say, there are starving people in the world; there are diseases that need to be cured. Before trying to describe in more detail how our space program is contributing to the solution of our earthly problems, I will briefly relate a true story that is a favorite of one of your countrymen, Dr. Ernst Stuhlinger, associate director of science at the Marshall Space Flight Center in Huntsville.

"Dr. Stuhlinger was born in Germany in 1913. He received his Ph.D. in physics from the University of Tuebingen in 1936. He was a member, as some of you may recall, of your country's rocket development team at Peenemünde headed by Wernher von Braun. He came to the U.S. in 1946, working for the U.S. Army at Fort Bliss, Texas. He moved to Huntsville in 1950, continuing his work at the Redstone Arsenal. Here's his story:

About 400 years ago there lived a count in a small town in Germany. He was one of the benign counts and he gave a large part of his income to the poor in his town. This was much appreciated because poverty was abundant during medieval times and there were epidemics of the plague, which ravaged the country frequently.

One day, the count met a strange man. He had a workbench and little laboratory in his house, and he labored hard during the daytime with menial work so he could afford a few hours every evening to work in his laboratory.

He ground small lenses from pieces of glass; he mounted the lenses in tubes and he used these gadgets to look at very small objects. The count was particularly fascinated by the tiny creatures that could be observed with the strong magnification, which nobody else had ever seen before.

The count invited the man to move with his laboratory to the castle, to become a member of the count's household and to devote henceforth all his time to the development and perfection of his optical gadgets as a special employee of the count.

The townspeople, however, became angry when they realized that the count was wasting his money, as they thought, on a stunt without purpose. 'We are suffering from this plague,' they said, 'while he is paying that man for a useless hobby!'

But the count remained firm. 'I give you as much as I can afford,' he said, 'but I will also support this man and his work, because I know that someday something will come out of it.'

"Indeed," says Nelson, "something very good came out of his work, and also out of similar work done by others at other places: the microscope. It is well known that the microscope has contributed more than any other invention to the progress of medicine, and that the elimination of the plague, and many other contagious diseases, is largely a result of studies which the microscope made possible.

"The count, by retaining some of his spending money for research and discovery, contributed far more to the relief of human suffering than he could have contributed by giving all his money to his plague-ridden community.

"Basic to the world's hunger problems are two functions: the production of food and the distribution of food. Food production by agriculture, cattle ranching, ocean fishing and other large-scale operations are efficient in some parts of the world, but drastically deficient in many others.

"For example, large areas of land could be utilized far better if efficient methods of watershed control, fertilizer use, weather forecasting, fertility assessment, plantation programming, field selection, planting habits, timing of cultivation, crop survey and harvest planning were applied.

"The best tool for the improvement of all these functions undoubtedly is the artificial earth satellite. Circling the globe at a high altitude, it can screen wide areas of land within a short time, it can observe and measure a large variety of factors indicating the status and conditions of crops, soil, droughts, rainfall, snow cover, etc., and it can radio this information to ground stations for appropriate use.

"It has been estimated that even a modest system of earth satellites equipped with earth resources sensors, working with a program for worldwide agricultural improvement, will increase the yearly crops by an equivalent of many billions of dollars.

"The distribution of the food to the needy is a completely different problem. The question is not so much one of shipping volume; it is one of international cooperation.

"The ruler of a small nation may feel very uneasy about the prospects of having large quantities of food shipped into his country by a large nation, simply because he fears that along with the food there may also be an import of influence and foreign power.

"Higher food production through survey and assessment from orbit and better food distribution through improved international relations, are only two examples of how profoundly the space program will impact life on earth.

"Every year, about a thousand technical innovations generated in the space program find their way into earthly technology where they lead to better medical instruments, better kitchen appliances and farm equipment, better sewing machines and radios, better ships and airplanes, better weather forecasting and storm warnings, better communications and better utensils and tools for everyday life."

I have not missed one cue as I follow his speech on paper and click the slides as the key word comes up.

"There are many needs" says Nelson, "but one of the greatest has to be more young men and women who choose science as a career. The space program with its wonderful opportunities to engage in truly magnificent research studies of moon and planets, of physics and astronomy, of biology and medicine is the ideal catalyst.

"How much human suffering can be avoided if nations, instead of competing in war, study the universe? Here's a slide that shows a view of our earth as seen from Apollo 8 when it orbited the moon last Christmas. Of all the many wonderful results of the space program so far, this picture may be the most important one. It opens our eyes to the fact that our earth is a beautiful and precious island in an unlimited void, and that there is no other place for us to live than the thin surface layer of our planet, bordered by the bleak nothingness of space. Ever since this picture was first published, voices have become louder and louder warning of the grave problems that confront us in our times: pollution, hunger, poverty, urban living, food production, water control, overpopulation.

"Fortunately, the space age not only holds out a mirror in which we can see ourselves, it also provides us with the technologies, the knowledge, the challenge, the motivation, and even the optimism to attack these tasks with confidence. What we learn in our space program, I believe, is fully supporting what Albert Schweitzer had in mind when he said, 'I am looking at the future with concern, but with good hope.'"

As Nelson ends his speech, I click the last slide, depicting the Saturn V on the launch pad. The Germans unanimously applaud and rise from their seats, each walking toward Nelson to shake his hand. I feel good about the speech I have written. Even though Nelson gets the applause, I feel it in my heart, and believe every word of it, too.

The aggressive German is heading my way. "Miss, may I speak with you one more time," he says. "I really want you to be with me tonight. What can I do to persuade you?"

Knowing our dog and pony show is over, I look him straight in the eyes and say, "Not a damn thing!"

. . . .

CHAPTER 15

IBM...READY FOR LAUNCH

Friday, July 11, 1969

Ountdown events began last night at 8 p.m. as the launch crews cleared the mobile launcher for installation of the command service module small ordnance. Today is T-5, five days until launch. The IU stage power is down and the launch crews are securing the vehicle's electrical support equipment. At T-66 hours, at 11 p.m. tonight, there will be a 12-hour built-in hold. During the countdown several "built-in holds" are scheduled. They serve two purposes: to give the launch crews a rest and if necessary replace any malfunctioning parts that might be revealed.

It's that time of the year in Florida when the residents are reminded that we live in the tropics. The mornings are hot and sticky and the afternoon thundershowers roll in like the tide. Today, it's already raining and it isn't even 8:30 a.m. The thunder is performing a percussion concert all around the Cape. The pace around the office has picked up; people are coming in earlier and staying later. Lunch hours are eliminated to meet schedules and to ensure that everyone will be ready for liftoff. I am putting the finishing touches on a press release regarding IBM's involvement in the launch when the phone startles me with its ring.

"Martha, I need you to cover the managers' meeting," says Warren. "Can you get over there right now?"

"Sure, no problem." I pick up my notebook and head to the control center. Nelson is standing at attention, waiting for everyone, next to the blackboard. On the blackboard is written: "System + People = Excellence." Clancy, Bob, and Pete are already in their seats chatting. Another 20 managers fill the room.

"Hell, I could piss in a coke bottle when I first came to the Cape, now I can't hit a bathtub," I overhear Don Crouger say to the trio. Don is known for his resistance to authority and his un-IBM ways. He is talented, but his bucking of management has gotten him into trouble more than a few times. He is short, with a reddish complexion and a receding hairline. I take my seat at the back of the room, while the managers occupy the seats around the giant mahogany table.

Nelson waits until the room is quiet, then begins. "If the systems are perfect then the people can screw up, and the systems, the process, will catch the error. It works in reverse too. If the people are perfect, then the systems might screw, but the people will catch any error.

"Gentlemen, we are five days from launch. We must be committed to perfection. Perfect systems, perfect people. It's up to you to prepare your people, to motivate them for this launch. Are any major problems confronting us at this time?"

Silence fills the room as each person waits for someone else to speak. No one speaks.

"Good," says Nelson. "All the world's eyes are on us."

MONDAY, JULY 14, 1969

This morning I'm putting the last touches on my article for *THINK MAGAZINE*. I begin the article:

IBM Cape Kennedy is "go" for Apollo 11 – Go for everything from critical launch preparations to special arrangements for IBMers visiting for the history-making liftoff this week.

"It's been a beautiful bird all the way through flight readiness testing," reports Robert Ehrhardt, Engineering manager of the Apollo/Saturn 506 vehicle, scheduled to soar moonward July 16.

"IBM's Saturn instrument unit has checked out perfectly as the onboard control system for the launch vehicle," he adds. "And all launch support equipment maintained and operated by IBM has been functioning smoothly.

"We're looking to another good launch, and another flawless IU performance in flight," says Ehrhardt.

As on-site launch preparations move toward the final countdown, a special off-site Apollo 11 task force is deep in final arrangements of another sort: making sure that being "at the Cape" for liftoff will be a richly memorable experience for IBM employees, and their families and guests.

Special displays, demonstrations, and souvenir brochures are developed for the facility's hospitality for an unprecedented number of IBMers and guests expected to pour in for liftoff. The task force deals with everything from traffic control and parking facilities to babysitters. There are employees assigned to find lodging accommodations, to give technical tours and provide women's activities. Just finding sleeping accommodations for hundreds of non-Cape IBMers who are taking advantage of the vacation season to travel to Florida with their families for the historic moon shot is a key assignment. Lodging availability questionnaires circulate among the local employees, producing a substantial reservoir of accommodations.

Arrangements to allow more wives and dependents of Cape Kennedy IBMers to view the launch than ever before, is another prime area of activity. In addition to reserving buses to carry dependents to viewing areas, three large fishing boats, one of which I will be on for launch, will provide an unobstructed vantage point for liftoff.

Our main administration building will remain open after working hours this week and next to enable employees and visitors to view the exhibits and presentations dealing with IBM's role in Apollo. Displays include models of the Saturn V vehicle, the instrument unit, as well as the lunar module, and photos of Apollo astronauts. Paintings, photographs and films depicting futuristic space concepts are displayed on the walls. Special Apollo 11 souvenir packets are being distributed to all employees today.

At 3 p.m., Clancy, Pete, Don, Ed and Bob report to their stations. At 5:30, the IU batteries are installed, and connected at 8:30 p.m. The ground computer is up and supporting with the IU stage power on through liftoff.

TUESDAY, JULY 15, 1969

At the Manned Flight Awareness reception, it is my job to escort the honoree and his wife around the reception and to make sure he is photographed with the astronauts as well as IBM's top management. The photos are then compiled in a keepsake album. The honoree is also awarded a three-day trip to any IBM or NASA location. Ken Clark is IBM's award winner.

I meet my local photographer, Don Black, whom we have hired to take photos. "We need to catch the astronauts first, they're only here for about an hour. Then they head over to NASA for a get-together. We can catch our own VIP's in the photo later," I say.

I scan the massive room, which is crammed with wall-to-wall people, shoulder-to-shoulder, with barely enough room to traverse it. Hundreds of contractor and NASA personnel line up to enter and then queue at the bars. I spot our honoree, Ken Clark, from Clancy's office, and his wife coming through the door.

"Hi, Ken," I begin as I maneuver my way through the throng.

"Martha, this is my wife, Karen," he says. "Sorry if I appear to be distant, but I've got other things on my mind. I'm scheduled to go to work in a couple of hours to support the launch. I have a very important meeting scheduled with Rocco Petrone at 11 p.m. Rocco is a harsh taskmaster who doesn't suffer fools, or anyone with a problem, lightly. His temper is legendary. I have no fear of Nelson, but I'm terrified of Petrone."

"I understand completely, Ken. We'll have you out of here in no time. Here comes my photographer, Don," I say, and then I introduce them.

We politely shake hands and I continue, "Just follow my lead and we'll begin your photography session. It will be fast, so try to keep up. It's all right to get a drink, but we don't want any drinks to appear in our photos. The astronauts will start showing up any minute so we'll grab as many as we can and start shooting. After the reception, you're invited to go to a private dinner here in the hotel with all of our top executives. No photos will be taken there."

A buzz goes through the crowd as all eyes focus on the doors. Someone in the crowd turns and says, "The Apollo 10 astronauts are here." I have memorized all the flights and their assigned crews. I mentally identify the trio as Tom Stafford, Eugene Cernan and John Young. They are all known to be friendly and helpful.

"Let's go," I say to Don, Ken and his wife. "We've got to be aggressive and get in line."

The astronauts are bombarded with requests for autographs and photos. The cameras click and flash away on a steady basis as the crew makes their way through the room. I finally reach Gene Cernan, introduce our honoree and myself, and ask permission to take his photo. Cernan is gracious and accommodating, asking Ken what he has done to be honored. Ken, as much he can in a short time, fills him in on his actions that earned him the award.

I then corner both Stafford and Young, who are equally cooperative. After the photos, we wait for more astronauts to arrive, filling the minutes with photos of me and some of the executives.

"Will Mr. Watson be attending?" asks Ken.

"Not to my knowledge. I understand he's flying in very early tomorrow morning in the company jet."

Another rash of flashbulbs go off as more astronauts enter the room. I strain to see the crew and recognize Andy, Tom and Bucky. After more than ten minutes, I see Andy coming towards us, handsomely dressed in a dark suit.

"This must be the IBM honoree," he says much to my surprise.

"Yes, sir," I answer. "This is Ken Clark and his wife, Karen."

"Congratulations, Ken," says Andy. "You're really making a great contribution to our program. I can tell you that no one appreciates your dedication more than the flight crews."

"Thank you very much," says Ken, beaming.

"How are you, Marth?" Andy asks as he uses his nickname for me.

"Very well, Andy. And you?"

"Busy, as was predicted. Nice to see you again," he responds.

My heart is beating fast as our eyes meet in a wonderful point of private contact where only the two of us share its secrets. Then Andy moves back into the crowd.

"WOW!" exclaims Ken. "Do you know him?"

"Yes, we've had occasion to meet a few times. He's a great guy."

WEDNESDAY, JULY 16, 1969

I know the procedures by heart. I have edited and typed them into the launch countdown plan and the launch communications plan. I can follow each step: At T-8 hours and 15 minutes, at 12:17 a.m., the launch support crew begins fueling procedures for the massive Saturn V vehicle, which concludes at 4:54 a.m. At 6:25 the astronauts plug themselves into portable oxygen containers and depart the Manned Spacecraft operations building. By the time I get to work at 7 a.m. the astronauts have already entered the spacecraft.

More than a million people are crowded into the Cape area to watch the launch of Apollo 11. There are people in campers and tents alongside the roads; others sleep on the beach, while thousands are in boats anchored in the Indian and Banana Rivers. Traffic is bumper-to-bumper from Titusville to the north and south through Patrick Air Force Base.

Clancy, Pete, Don, Bob, our test conductor, Ed, as well as IBM's entire 1200 member team, even those who are officially off duty since they've already worked one shift, are standing by for the final hours before liftoff.

It is predicted that a billion people around the world are glued to their television sets for the event that no one wants to miss.

Ken Clark, responsible for troubleshooting and repairing in as near real-time as possible any ground computer software problems, takes his seat among the 20-member IBM launch team in Firing Room 1. They look out through the blast-proof windows at the Saturn V standing proudly on Launch Pad 39A in the Florida sun in front of the Banana River. Clancy sits at his console in Firing Room 2 while NASA director Rocco Petrone sits in front of the firing room, overlooking the entire launch team, made up of NASA and the contractor reps. In the glass visitors' room sits Wernher von Braun, the German scientist who brought his dreams and his team to America.

Onboard the spacecraft, the astronauts perform their readiness checks. In their personal kits, according to Andy, they carry prayers, poems, medallions, coins, flags, envelopes, brooches, tiepins, insignia, cuff links, rings, and even one diaper pin. The only criteria are that the objects have to be small. Mike Collins, the press release says, carries a small hollow bean, less than a quarter of an inch long, which holds fifty elephants, carved from slivers of ivory.

Bolted to a leg of the lunar module is one of the few items the crew will leave behind, a plaque with the words: *Here Men from Planet Earth First Set Foot Upon the Moon, July 1969 a.d. We Came for Peace for all Mankind.* President Nixon signed it.

The launch is proceeding despite the demonstration from Abernathy's black activists group, despite warnings from the man in Israel who tells of the dangers from gigantic ants that infest the moon. "It would be a disaster," he says, "if the LM comes down on one of the giant anthills."

I leave the building at 7:30 a.m. with four high-ranking IBMers from division headquarters, and one female employee, also from Gaithersburg. The woman, a very close friend of Nelson's, has flown down on the Corporate jet with other executives, much to the embarrassment and condemnation of corporate. Still, I like her. She is warm, friendly, unassuming and attractive. I do not feel the need to judge anyone and I refrain from even going there in my thoughts. It takes more than 40 minutes to make our way to the boats docked at the locks in Port Canaveral. An hour later more than 300 VIPs are gathered for a front row seat in the boats we've leased for the day. Once onboard, coffee, pastries and fruit await each group. From the sounds coming from the other non-IBM boats, more than coffee is being served. Guests have their cameras hung around their necks on this hot, summer day. A gentle breeze over the water floats by the boats, making them probably the coolest spots to view the launch. The engines start and we begin our trip to the Banana River, which takes about an hour. Once in place, our anchor is dropped, and we pass the time by getting acquainted as the radio blasts out NASA's countdown sequence.

It is now T-30 minutes and counting...IBM's instrument unit power transfer test has been successfully completed and the Lunar Module has switched over to internal power.

A cheer goes up among our group, knowing that IBM is now in control of the launch and its maneuvers that will lead it to the moon. My thoughts are on the men and women of IBM who are at their stations: Clancy, Bob, Pete, and Ken, as well as

Ed, who at the appropriate moment will give IBM's commitment to launch.

Has there ever been a larger engineering feat for America? Other than America's past wars, has there ever been more personal sacrifices put into a goal? Has there ever been a technical team who responded with such dedication, and under a timeline that added even more pressure? I think of the massive hours of three different shifts, the lost weekends, lost marriages, the drinking, the affairs, the lost lives. This team has endured it all and the payoff is about to happen.

T-6 minutes, and counting...the space vehicle is in final status checks and the destruct system has been armed. The IU's Inertial Platform has been positioned to the final launch azimuth.

Neither the Function Executor patch nor keyboard workaround are needed.

I can visualize the press site where Thomas J. Watson, Jr. sits with the other VIP's awaiting the final countdown. In my thoughts, I can see Ed in the firing room, his eyes glancing at the closed circuit TV monitor where sheets of frozen fuel drift off the booster. I know that it's at this point where the first stage test conductor will give a GO, followed by the second and third stage test conductors, each uttering their company's commitment. Ed will finally speak in a loud, clear, positive voice, "IBM is GO for launch." The lunar module TC will then echo a GO, followed by the TC's for the service module, command module, and the launch escape tower...and lastly, the astronauts, who will give the final GO.

T-3 minutes, and counting...The firing command has been initiated; the automatic terminal count sequence has begun. All systems are GO.

Those in the firing room hear Wernher von Braun repeat the Lord's Prayer out loud as everyone bows their heads with him.

"Good luck and Godspeed," says NASA's Paul Donnelly to the astronauts. Armstrong replies, "Thank you very much. We know it'll be a good flight."

T-50 seconds, and counting...Oxidizer tanks in the upper stages are now pressurized. Transfer has occurred to internal power for the entire launch vehicle.

Several women on the boat squeal with excitement. "This is it," someone with binoculars yells. I say a silent prayer. I know the swing-arms will pull away at T-12 seconds.

T-8 seconds, and counting...The ignition sequence has been started.

From my vantage point I spot the golden flames from the massive engines, as millions of eyes focus on the pad, waiting for upward movement.

T-2 seconds, and counting…First stage engines running.

I know that the hold-down arms will hold the vehicle in place until full power is achieved. They will release at exactly T-0.

Liftoff, we have liftoff at 9:32 a.m.

There is no immediate sound connected with the rise of the vehicle from our viewpoint. Everyone cheers as the emblem of American ingenuity rises higher and higher, leaving vapor trails as beautiful as the bird itself. It rises over the trees, the buildings and into the clouds. Finally the sound travels to our boats, making them bob in the water. Everyone is hugging each other. I can't stop smiling. So much has been given, so much lost. But today, all the dreams come true.

It's been 2,974 days since John F. Kennedy asked the United States to commit itself to a lunar landing. Today, we have launched Apollo 11, 169 days before his deadline. The launch team has met their part of the goal. Now, it is up to the astronauts and Houston to continue the mission.

The IU performs meticulously, initiating all stage separations and course maneuvers heading it to the moon until T+4 hours and 10 minutes at which time the IU separates from the command and lunar modules. The IU initiates its last maneuver, instructing the S-IVB into a propellant dump and 'slingshot' operation to send the IU into solar orbit.

With the launch successfully accomplished, all the boats speed back to land so we can find the nearest television sets to follow the journey to the moon. After more than an hour, our boats return to Port Canaveral.

Later that day, lunch is hosted and the tab picked up personally by Thomas J. Watson, Jr. IBMers storm into the huge Hilton convention room to hear Mr. Watson's words of praise. Elation fills the air as employees exchange launch location stories and find their seats. A respectful hush fills the auditorium as Mr. Watson takes the podium.

"I cannot begin to tell you how proud I am of what our team has accomplished here today. I've heard about the long hours, the tragedies, and the relentless pursuit of this goal of launching men to the moon. I've heard incredible tales of teamwork that sets standards for the world itself.

"I've had an interest in aeronautics for some time, being a pilot myself. I know how crucial it is to have all your systems in perfect order to fly. But, to tell you the truth, when I hear about all the hundreds of thousands of systems that must be perfect for a mission, it is mindboggling. My hat goes off to each and every one of you. I was determined to be here today. I wouldn't have missed it under any circumstances.

"I won't take any more of your time. I know many of you have been working straight through for several days. I want to make one announcement. Monday, July 21st, the day lunar exploration begins, will be a holiday for all IBMers at this location and in Huntsville. Enjoy the day; rest on your laurels and again, thank you for your dedication to this national goal."

That was it. No long prepared speech but an off the cuff, down to earth "thank you." It is the ultimate "thank you" as far as the employees are concerned. Having Mr. Watson recognize your work is high enough reward.

.

CHAPTER 16

. . . .

APOLLO 12 THROUGH 17

Before Apollo 11 launches, the peak employment at KSC exceeds 26,000: after Apollo 11, KSC begins to reduce manpower. By the end of 1970, we are around 15,000.

As each Apollo astronaut crew trains together for more than a year, it appears that they each develop their own crew personalities, with the blending of three distinct individuals who learn to think and react as one. Workers gossip about each crew and their dedication to the mission. Collectively, say some who work closely with the crew, the astronauts know the vehicle as well as the technicians and engineers who fabricate and assemble it.

Apollo 11 was our show and tell. It proved our ability to go to the moon and return. The missions after Apollo 11 begin the many science tests and experiments.

IBMers man their consoles in the Firing Room (IBM)

Charles Conrad, Richard Gordon and Alan Bean, all Navy men, are at the helm of Apollo 12, or Yankee Clipper and Intrepid. On the eve of the Apollo 11 launch, the Intrepid test team verifies the lunar module sub-systems. Another group tests the command and service modules, changing out fuel cells in Apollo. A suspect component in IBM's instrument unit is removed for special testing in Owego and returns a week later.

September 1969 brings major changes in management both at NASA and our IBM facility. Dr. Rocco Petrone leaves the launch director's post

Another launch, another Facility Dinner Show

to become Apollo Program Director at NASA Headquarters. Walter Kapryan succeeds him. Dr. Kurt Debus remains as KSC director.

Joanne comes into my office with an announcement for immediate release. "I just wrote this up for our bulletin," she says. As I look it over I realize the huge impact.

"This is big," I say.

"Yes, Nelson is being promoted and transferring to Gaithersburg, and our own Bob, from our chorus and the head of all engineering, is assuming the reins as manager of our facility," she says.

"Everyone loves Bob. I don't think he has one enemy," I add. "He'll do a great job."

Word quickly spreads with positive feedback. Everyone is pleased that Bob is awarded this top position. He is a skilled engineer, easy to work with, humble and down to earth. Gone are the verbal screams and intimidations from Nelson.

Weeks later there is a more relaxed atmosphere now with Bob running the show. With the first successful moon landing behind us we let out a collective sigh of relief.

Countdown for launch of Apollo 12 commences at 8 a.m. on November 7, 1969. Four holds are built into the count, allowing time for problem solving. NASA reports that a problem develops at T-40 hours when one of the two hydrogen tanks fails to chill down when the extremely cold liquid propellant is pumped aboard. The suspect tank is replaced with one designated for Apollo 13. Technicians work around the clock to make the substitution and the countdown proceeds. At T-24 hours the crew surprises the launch team, by flying their T-38 jets across KSC as a salute to all of us working below.

Overnight heavy rains fall intermittently all across central Florida. Two aircraft fly through the clouds assuring NASA that there is no lightning present. The word is out among the workers that President and Mrs. Nixon are at the north side of the VAB, joining approximately 4,000 observers. Apollo 12 lifts off from the pad at 11:22 a.m. on November 14, 1969.

I am watching from the press site as Apollo 12 disappears into the clouds. At the 36-second mark, a gasp goes through the crowd as we see two flashes of lightning streak ground-ward on either side of the launch tower. Later it is explained in a NASA press release that the power outage causing the fuel cell, lights, and bus overloads compares to no more than a fuse blowout in a home.

The crew logs in 244 hours and 36 minutes of flight time. They are put into quarantine at the Manned Spacecraft Center in Houston upon their return. As I hear it, they are scheduled for a world tour but the crew insists that their first visit will be to KSC for a reunion with the launch team. On December 17, 1969, I hurry out to the VAB and find my seat as the crew thanks us for our role in the successful mission.

Apollo 12 Commander Charles Conrad takes the podium and says, "The crew didn't consider the flight over until we got back here. We forgive the weatherman for his job but had we to do it again, I'd launch under the same conditions. We had such fine equipment that when you add up the little difficulties we came up with on the flight, it wouldn't fill a half page of paper.... I'd just like to tell you ... you all did a hell of a job for us."

Dick Gordon stands and says, "The real guts of these flights, after their formative opening stages, are really put together here. The hardware is brought here, it's mated here...this is really our home."

Later, Apollo 13 becomes the showstopper. Preparations for the Apollo 13 mission begin in June 1969. The initial crew includes James Lovell as commander, Thomas Mattingly and Fred Haise.

According to NASA's updates, the loaded vehicle moves to Pad A in December 1969. A strange thing happens during the countdown demonstration test. A large quantity of liquid oxygen used to chill down the liquid oxygen pumping system on the booster stage is emptied into a drainage ditch outside the pad perimeter fence. This, I learned in safety training, is a routine fueling procedure. It is now March 1970 and there's a chill in the air and no wind. The dense oxygen fog builds up in the ditch and overflows into a nearby roadway. A three-car security team, maybe including ruddy-man, clears the pad area and turns on his ignition, a loud pop and flames spring from beneath his hood. In rapid succession, the other two cars burst into flames. They all run for cover. After almost an hour the oxygen cloud dissipates and the fire is brought under control.

The incident, I learn through the Cape Vine, the gossip link among KSC workers, causes KSC officials to extend the drainage pipes beyond the perimeter ditch into a marshy area further from the pad. Another incident pops up in the number 2 liquid oxygen tank in the service module. One of the two liquid oxygen tanks that feed the fuel cells, which supply electrical power and life support systems on the Apollo, fails to empty completely during repeated tests. Only by energizing the tank's heater and venting the tank are the crews able to empty its contents.

Word spreads through the Cape Vine that Charlie Duke, a member of the backup crew, has come down with measles. Tests are run on the others, which reveal that everyone else has immunity, except Mattingly. On April 10, it is announced that John Swigert will replace Mattingly because it would be unwise to risk the possibility that the command module pilot might develop measles during the mission, particularly when he will pilot Odyssey around the Moon alone while his crewmates are on the lunar surface.

The count begins at 4:13 a.m. on April 11. Liftoff occurs on schedule, at 2:13 p.m., the IU executes staging and directs the vehicle on its way to the moon flawlessly. Despite a few minor problems, the flight proceeds with gratifying smoothness.

I hurry into the control center to watch the mission on TV as well as to hear the NASA link. It is 55 hours into the mission. The crew is entering the lunar module, Aquarius. We all are relaxed, watching the telecast from space, which lasts about 30 minutes. We're all smiling. Jones is seated next to me and Bob Ehrhardt is talking to Clancy Boswell.

"Houston, we've got a problem here!" says one of the crew. We all stop in our tracks, "Did you hear that? There's a problem," says Bob.

Even though it's not an IBM problem, it is a problem. We operate as a family, as one unit in the Apollo program. We all want one thing: success for the mission and the safety and lives of our astronauts.

NASA relays the situation: Liquid oxygen tank number 2 in the service module—the tank found defective during ground tests—has exploded, wiping out the fuel cells that supply life-sustaining oxygen and electrical power for the command and service modules. The backup batteries can only supply power for 10 hours and the carbon dioxide levels in the command module are rising to dangerous levels.

"Wow," says Bob, "a flat tire 87 hours from home."

Through the next hours, NASA performs at its highest peak gathering experts to come up with solutions to the life-threatening problems. Now, with a plan developing to move the astronauts from the command module to the lunar module for the trip around the moon and back, providing hope, the various contractors between KSC and Houston go to work.

We receive printed updates regularly on each phase of the work needed to overcome the anomalies. A KSC team, made up of contractor engineers, includes test conductor Bill Rezanka, who verifies that none of the Instrument Unit systems had anything to do with the problem. The Houston team then devises a means of recharging the command module's re-entry batteries from the lunar module's electrical system. Another KSC recommendation turns off the radar heaters to save electricity. Rockwell and Grumman engineers help devise ways to transfer water from the portable life support systems into the lunar module's water coolant system.

KSC engineers, duplicating solutions tested at Houston, verify the procedure for removal of carbon dioxide from the command module. This allows the flight crew to duplicate the procedure, immediately returning the cabin to tolerable levels.

Later, as I'm working at my desk, one of our quality assurance guys stops in my office. I notice he's holding something in his hand. I know him vaguely from the chorus but have not had much contact with him.

"Hi, Howard," I say looking up from my work. "What can I do for you?"

"I've just recently found out about a wonderful new gadget. It stretches one's penis. I've been using it. See the results," he says as he hands me a nude photograph of himself, featuring a stretched out skinny penis, probably a foot long.

I take one look and yell at him, "What the hell do you think you're doing bringing that photo in here to me. I don't want to see your screwed up penis. Now get out of here before I call Bob Jones. You don't want to lose your job over a stupid incident like this!"

He turns and runs down the hall, fear on his face. I sit down and my face is burning red, my teeth grinding. I get up and stomp into Joanne's office and tell her what has just happened. She laughs and asks me what I said to him. I told her.

"You should have laughed at the photo," she says.

"It wasn't a laughing matter. The guy was serious. What did he expect me to say?"

"Probably, that you're really impressed and when can we get together."

"Ugh, the thought convulses me. It is the height of disrespect as far as I'm concerned," I answer.

"Well, look at it this way. You're not one of the astronauts facing a huge crisis, not knowing if you're going to make it back to Earth alive. Get over it," she says, "and get on with the day." And I do.

When the crew returns to KSC, 7,000 employees, including Joanne and I, greet them in the transfer aisles of the VAB. Lovell tells us, "We're proud to come back today and tell you, 'thank you.' I think the mission matured the space program a little, because people were perhaps getting a bit complacent about what we do."

I laugh when he says this, as do all the workers around me. No time for complacency at KSC, and certainly no time to look at obscene Polaroid photos.

Jack and I seem to be a solid couple, that is, we've been together now more than five years. We spend weekends together, play tennis with Pinky and John, and neither one of us dates anyone else. Sometimes we go to Orlando, Tampa, or to Vero Beach's John's Island for a couple's retreat, the girls staying with their Dad. We go to the movies or dance to *Proud Mary*, as the band plays at the Eau Gallie Yacht Club after Shrimp and Suds on Friday nights. We dress up as Raggedy Ann and Andy for the Halloween costume party. He drinks beer, I don't and he respects my wishes.

Every Wednesday after work we play doubles together with two other guys, a judge and a tire salesman, then head to the Surf Restaurant for dinner. He follows me home and spends the night and leaves early the next morning.

I love that I have someone who listens to me. He's someone I can easily share my desires, disappointments and challenges, without fear of judgment or advice. We also have a good physical relationship which I never tire of, never wanting to abstain from his needs.

He calls me most days and when he doesn't, I worry. He doesn't give me 100 percent, but 80 percent is about it. Still I don't feel he's mature enough to be a stepfather to my girls, nor do I think he wants to be. Funny, when we women fall in love, we sometimes seem to magnify the good things about our men and hide their shortcomings. He belittles some of my physical attributes; doesn't care for my feet, my breasts are not big enough for him. Still, I hold on to the possibility that this is THE guy. He makes my heart sing...but then again, I allow him to make my heart sing. I've given him permission. And, he's never once told me he loves me, which is hard for me to take.

He usually takes a vacation without me, going to a singles club in the islands. Once when he is away on a trip, I miss him desperately. When he calls upon his return, I can hardly wait to see him. I watch from the window when his car drives up. He stays in the car, listening to music, pondering what to say to me, I imagine, or how to act. It is a strange feeling, a sixth sense that perhaps this relationship has run its course.

I think we create our own concept of being in love. We create that perfect person who in our imagination and desire becomes our Prince Charming, to fulfill all our dreams. We see in our guy more than he is or can be. It is our own thoughts that give wings to ecstasy and fulfillment. We are mesmerized by what should be, instead of what really is, because we want it to be so.

I've had all the children I want to have. Jack has never had any, nor has he ever been married. I make a monumental decision to have the Band-Aid surgery to have my tubes tied. It is the best decision for me, not for Jack. It is a simple procedure performed as an outpatient. At the same time, I'm to have a Morton's neuroma removed from my foot. I have the procedure performed on a Thursday, with the idea of returning to work on Monday morning. I drive myself to and from the surgery. I recover on my own, except for the loving attention from my girls. Jack neither calls, nor comes by to help. My decision and his absence speaks volumes about our future.

At work, Bob Ehrhardt proves to be an excellent IBM facility manager. We've had no crises and harmony reigns, or so it seems, until one morning Bob Jones comes around to each department and announces: "I'm sorry to report to you that Bob Ehrhardt's only daughter has been found dead in her bed this morning. She was 16. She had a wisdom tooth extracted yesterday, went to a party last night and never woke up this morning."

Everyone in my department is in shock and the room fills with the sound of gasps. No other pain could possibly be harder than losing a child. Bob Jones knows exactly what Ehrhardt is going through. It was only last year that he was called out of a meeting when word came that one of his sons had fallen off a mountain while climbing in Switzerland and had died.

The funeral is held in a couple of days. As many as can, attend the very sad service. I look around and see IBMers who are working the night shift, supposed to be sleeping now, attending. The countdown for

Apollo 14 begins tomorrow. Out of great love and support for Bob and his wife, Betty, the church is filled to capacity.

We mingle outside the church, trying to make some sense of a young girl's death. I turn and ask Jo: "Have they found out what caused her death yet?"

"You know how exacting Bob is. He was out all day yesterday, asking questions of the dentist and the kids at the party. It turns out it was a typical teenage party, a little beer, that's all. The dentist called it anaphylactic shock. The mixture of the beer with the painkiller could have stopped her heart. Another theory is Hepatitis C."

"It's hard to accept no matter what the cause," says Joanne.

That evening I cover the Manned Flight Awareness reception. I finally get to meet Wernher von Braun, the handsome, tall father of our space program. I also meet movie star and Air Force Colonel Jimmy Stewart.

The next morning the countdown begins. Bob Ehrhardt, ever the dedicated soldier, is at his post at 0600.

The time flies by at work—we go through the perfect launches of Apollo 14 through 17. Andy completes his moon mission as commander, being one of the few who actually walks on the moon.

Apollo 15 astronauts place a microfilm capsule of the Apollo MFA honorees on the moon with 11 IBM awardees, including Ken Clark and Gary Gustafson.

As we leave the Apollo moon program, which culminates in perfect launches and missions, we transition to Apollo/Skylab and then Apollo Soyuz with the Russians. The years have flown by, almost eight and one-half years for me. There are only a few of us IBMers left, a skeleton crew; most have already transferred to other facilities. Even Warren has been transferred, leaving me as the lone IBM writer. Warren and I become very good friends during this time. I miss him today. It was only in the beginning that he tried to wear me down, but then his mission was to mold me, as he understood it.

Apollo provided a time of peace and glory in America. In the 60's we were a nation mistrusting our government after two wars and the assassination of our president. Apollo was our guiding light to something not just America could bond over, but the whole world. I remember watching the news broadcasts of people all over the world watching as we landed on the moon, cheering on our astronauts. Twenty-four Americans orbited the moon. Twelve walked on its surface. Six drove lunar vehicles. Thousands worked on Apollo, from secretaries, typists, technicians, programmers, analysts, engineers and even writers. Thousands committed their lives to this project, some paying dearly. The halls are pretty quiet now, almost eerie, without the old crowds scurrying around.

Jack and I break up. Seems he's now dating one of the girls I introduced him to as my doubles partner. She works as a flight controller at Patrick. It is the most depressing time of my life. I've seen my friends at work leave one by one. Lost the love of my life and now my job on the space program is coming to an end.

I embrace the positive teachings of Christian Science, calling a practitioner for help. He assures me that "Good is still unfolding." He asks me to do one thing first before anything else.

"Make a gratitude list of what you're grateful for these past years. They can't be material, they have to be spiritual things," he says.

I start my list by being grateful for my family. The fact that I've succeeded as a single mother; the wonderful progress I've made in my work; the loving friends who have helped me along the way. I'm grateful for the intelligence that I reflect, the deeper understanding of love, not just human love, but divine love that is never depleted.

What I've learned over these past years is who I am, and what I want. I've put myself out there to discover and explore, to find answers. I've endured pain, but found joy. I've learned how smart I am by studying and learning. I'm not going to settle for less than I deserve in a job, or in relationships.

If I were to sit down right now with one of my heroines from literature, Scarlett O'Hara, the conversation would go something like this:

"So Scarlett, you say you're not even going to think about your troubles until tomorrow. I'm with you on that one. I'm not going to worry about anything because women like us we know what we can do. We don't dread tomorrow, we embrace it, looking for that rainbow that we create … all by ourselves."

Grand finale for our last show for Apollo 17

It was a great ride!

CHAPTER 17

. . . .

1975...WE MARCH...

The Apollo program, Skylab and Soyuz, is coming to an end. There is nothing else. Funding has come to an end. America has lost interest. The IBM offices will be closing this coming week.

There is one thing I must do before my job ends and I start hitting the pavement trying to find another company to hire me. I know they'll all want me to begin as a secretary but I'm holding firm...I'm a writer.

Today, I'm heading back to my hometown of Ft. Lauderdale to visit my mother, who is wheelchair bound. She doesn't get out of the house very much. She and my Dad live in a small, modest one-bedroom apartment in Wilton Manors. I called her yesterday and told her I would be by to pick her up.

"It will be good to see you, Sugar," she says.

Earthrise says it all...we are one! (NASA)

"I've got a surprise for you. We're going to a special place and do a very special thing," I explain.

"What are we going to do?" She asks.

"It wouldn't be a surprise if I told you. But, trust me, it's something that you'll enjoy. Something I read about in the paper."

As I pull up to the house and park, I remember the time when my mother almost died. When she was racked with so much pain from a botched procedure that her life almost slipped away. It was at that moment I saw the incredibly hard decision she had to make...and the courage it took to go through with it. I remember a time when women had no birth control, no say in what they could do with their own bodies, or how much their bodies could endure.

The astronaut crews always returned to the VAB to thank us (NASA)

I know my mother never talked about it, never confided in anyone and doesn't even know that my sister and I figured it all out so many years ago.

I knock on the door and walk right in. I see the smiling faces of my Dad and Mom, who have been patiently waiting for me, knowing that my visit will be the highlight of their day, week and probably their month. I hug my Dad first and then lean over to kiss my Mom on her cheek as she sits in her wheelchair. She is pale, and using one of my Mom's own sayings, "just skin and bones." Every finger of my mother's two hands is crooked at every joint, pointing in different directions. Even her hands turn aside, rather than point forward. I think the arthritis has burned out, the majority of the tremendous pain she experienced during the onset subsided, leaving the scars of deformity. Her knees, though, still swell and ache, as do her feet.

I spend some time just chatting. We talk about their favorite TV shows. I go to the refrigerator for some cold water and notice the stains in the sink. I look under the sink and find the Comet cleanser and clean the sink, knowing that just this simple task is beyond my mother's capability and my Dad really doesn't even notice it. My brother Hersch lives nearby and visits every day for lunch, helping with whatever they might need. He should be arriving soon so I continue cleaning, taking the Comet into the bathroom and tackling the sink, toilet and bathtub.

My Dad is dressed the way he's always dressed. He wears a plaid shirt, with his tie tucked in-between the four and fifth buttons. I tidy their room and straighten the drawers. Inside one drawer I find Christmas presents that I sent for the past several holidays still in the boxes, tissue paper still around new ties and shirts for my Dad, nightgowns and robes for my mother.

"Mom," I ask, "why are my Christmas presents still in the boxes? Why aren't you wearing them?"

"They're just too fancy. Too much sugar for a dime," she replies in yet another southern saying.

I hear Hersch enter the house and start calling to me by my childhood name. "Boppa, are you here?"

I answer with the name he absolutely forbids me to use anymore but this is the one occasion I can say it.

"Yes, Junior, I'm in here." As I walk out of the bedroom, I see by the sack in his arms that he's brought sandwiches for our lunch.

"I've got ham and cheese, or roast beef and Swiss and root beer to drink," he says as he puts everything down. "Someone's been cleaning. Looks great."

As we sit around the small room that serves as both the living room and kitchen, we eat our lunches; I ask Hersch how his job is going at the Sun Sentinel, where he works in advertising.

"It's going good. I now have all the banks as my customers."

"How's your karate?" I ask.

"Good. I've got a tournament this weekend. Oh my god, I forgot to tell you. I met Chuck Norris the other day and had lunch with him. Our movie critic, Roger Hurlburt, was doing a lunchtime interview with him and invited me. Great guy!" says Hersch.

My Dad turns the TV on so he can catch the noon news. We finish our lunch and I clear the plates. There is no dishwasher so I wash the plates as soon as I get them to the kitchen. I dry the plates and put them in the cabinet.

"Well, it's time for Mom and me to leave," I say. "Can you give me a hand getting her into the car, Hersch?"

"I'm not going unless you tell me where we're going!" my Mom demands.

"Then it won't be a surprise," I say, holding the door open as my brother, who already knows our destination, grabs Mom in her wheelchair and backs it out the door. "Just trust me, Mom."

I kiss my Dad goodbye and tell him we'll be back in a couple of hours. Even he doesn't know where we're heading.

Hersch helps Mom into the front seat and puts the wheelchair in my trunk.

"Thanks, Hersch. Love you."

"Love you. Let me know how it goes," he says.

We drive north to Boca, just north of Palmetto Parkway, the east side of Federal Highway to a small park. I get as close as I can with the car since Mom doesn't have a special sticker indicating her disability. I offered to get her one but she would have no part in calling herself disabled.

There's a traffic jam with all the cars cramming into the area, searching for parking. I go to the trunk and pull out my mother's wheelchair and struggle to get it put together. Two women stop. One says: "Let me help you. My mother has a chair just like this." She flips a few things and opens it immediately.

"Thank you so much," I say.

"No, thank you for coming today."

I get Mom to stand. She does so but I hear her moans that tell me how difficult the task is for her. I fasten the strap around her and we get on our way.

As we travel about two blocks I finally tell my Mom the purpose of today's trip.

"Mom, we're going to march for pro-choice today. I'm going to push you all the way, you and me, and all these other wonderful women," I say and watch her face as the tears start to flow down her cheeks. I stop the wheelchair, put on the brakes and get in front of her.

"I know you'd never want any other woman to go through what you did," I say.

"You knew, all this time? It was the most difficult thing I ever had to do, but I was in such constant pain," she explains.

"I know, Mom. Every woman deserves to have a choice, even if it is difficult, don't you think?"

"Yes, I do, Sugar. They should be able to have a real doctor, too."

"Okay, then, let's go."

We get in one of the lines and someone announces over a loud speaker, "Welcome, Sisters. Today, we march to let our voices be heard. Please begin." We walk for about a mile. Pushing the wheelchair isn't difficult. Several women offer to help but I refuse. It is my honor to push my mother today. She epitomizes what women have had to go through. She is living proof of the need for abortion rights. Placards with the words *Abortion Rights for All and We Want Choice* are all around us. One gal offers me one and I give it to my mother. She tries to hold it with both her hands but settles on placing it between her arms, the only way she can hold most things. She holds it as high as she can, and as proudly as she can, finally smiling and enjoying the day and what it means for all women.

When we return to the park, we find seats as the guest speaker fills us in on the future of the subject that has brought us here today. I watch my mother's face as she listens intently to every word and surveys the crowd around us. After the speaker finishes, she comes over to the wheelchair and talks to Mom.

"Tell me your story," she says to my mother.

"I was 27 when the arthritis stuck me. I had four children, lost one prematurely. I was in such constant pain in my feet, I couldn't stand and my hands were so bad I couldn't hold much. I couldn't imagine going through a pregnancy and then taking care of an infant. I had no other choice. I had the procedure from some idiot and almost died," says my mother, who speaks of the incident for the first time in her life.

"And I'm sure you want a future that offers a choice," says the speaker.

"Yes, I do. It's a wonderful thing for all these women to come together, walk together like this and talk about it. It's unbelievable," says my mother.

After the march ends, we stay around another half hour as other women gravitate towards the wheelchair and thank my mother for participating. It's probably more talking than she's done in the past year.

I drive my mother home and help her into the house.

"Herschell," she says to my Dad, "You won't believe where Martha took me. We were in a parade for women's rights. Can you believe that?"

"Well, that's just fine, Nellie. I'm so glad you did that," he says.

I stay another hour, my Mom telling Dad all the people she met and the conversations she had. I stand to leave.

"Martha," says my mother, "Thank you. I loved it."

"Sure Mom, I knew you would."

The next day, as I drive to work for the last time, my last drive through Patrick Air Force Base...the last time I walk through the back doors of the IBM offices in Cape Canaveral...the end of my IBM career...the culmination of the Apollo, Skylab and Soyuz Programs—my heart is pounding, my eyes moist. It's been a few months shy of nine years doing a job I would have paid them for—writing about the engineers, the analysts, programmers, test conductors, secretaries and the executives... the IBM Apollo launch support team.

I've had a front row seat to the greatest engineering, man-made endeavor ever accomplished on Earth, achieved by a team that went way beyond what anyone thought possible: Launch men to the moon and bring them back safely.

I get to my desk and see several boxes placed in my room. I know what they are for...to pack up my things.

IBM offers me a job in Owego, New York. I've been there twice for writing assignments, once in May and the other time in October and it was, by my Florida standards, winter both times. There is no way a Florida girl can handle the cold, the snow and to be so far away from my ocean. I decline the transfer, which means a voluntary exit. Thanks, but no thanks.

IBM's strong policy to secure and offer transfers to all its salaried employees comes through for everyone. Employees who work for other contractors are not so fortunate. I don't feel sorry for myself; I have achieved my goal of progressing into a writer. I have progressed, not only as a writer, but also as a woman.

It is the technical team, the engineers, analysts, programmers, who have been so carefully and diligently searched for, courted, employed and groomed for one-of-a-kind jobs, who I think of today. This combined team, after achieving an unbelievable goal within the 10-year limit set by Kennedy, performed in an exemplary manner. I think they are the greatest technological team ever assembled, achieving the most difficult challenge of all mankind. The names of the astronauts will forever be inscribed in our history books, but the names of the entire Apollo launch support team and the thousands that supported Apollo elsewhere will only be known to a few.

After packing up my things, I grab the box and head to my car in the parking lot. I open the back door and place my box, containing eight and a half years of memories, on the back seat. I take one look back at the building and say out loud, "Godspeed, Apollo team. I'll never forget you."

I am reminded of Neil Armstrong's famous lines when he took his first step on the moon, *"That's one small step for man; one giant leap for mankind."* I am brought back to a time when Mrs. Spaulding told me, *"You have 'The Step'…your step is concentrated and it hurries you along, guides you to win, or to accomplish. Your pace becomes a little faster; your stride is determined and strong, you become more focused."*

She told me I'd understand the complete message behind *'The Step'* and now I do understand. It's about commitment and focus. It's about fulfilling a dream, being so dedicated that your step becomes one with all the others.

We all had *'The Step.'* The entire Apollo team!

"We choose to go to the moon! We choose to go to the moon and do the other things, not because they are easy, but because they are hard, because that goal will serve to organize and measure the best of our energies and skills,

because that challenge is one we are willing to accept, one we are unwilling to postpone, and one we intend to win...."

John F. Kennedy

EPILOGUE

After about six months of being unemployed, Harris Corporation, in Melbourne, Florida, hired me as a PR writer. Harris is an engineering firm providing many different products, including communications equipment and specialty items for national intelligence. They have had products on every manned space flight America has had.

After two years I met my future husband, John Lemasters, senior vice president of the Satellite division at Harris Corporation. I wrote speeches for him, as well as numerous other PR items. He was married at the time and asked me to meet him for a drink. After all these years I knew my answer. "I don't go out with married men. You figure out your situation and if you ever leave your marriage, then you can call me."

He did seek a divorce. After which time I began dating him. We were married a year later. In a few years we left Melbourne when he accepted a job as president and CEO of a Fortune 500 company. We were married over 22 years. He was an unselfish person and a true southern gentleman.

After we married I retired from corporate work and became interested in women's issues, becoming president of The Women's Center in

IBM reunion April 2015. From left to right: Frank Penovich, NASA; Dot Gardner, Finance & Accounting; Ed Chandler, Test Operations; Sharon Witt, Executive secretary to the facility manager; Jim Handley, Manager, Systems Programming & Advanced Programs; Jack Cassidy, Martha Croskeys Lemasters, Communications; Charles Ernst, Bob Kirby, LVDC; Joanne Lauterbach Miller, Communications; Mary Jo Sloan, Communications; Joe Elder, IU Networks; Marylou Duffy, Personnel; Emma Jean McKinley (spouse), Alton McKinley, Instrumentation & Communications Department; Ken Clark, Saturn Ground Computer Software Support; Tom Santos, LVDC; Patrick Cuyno, Spacelab; Joe Harris, Guy Dryden, Dee-6; Gary Vaiskauckas, LPS; Hal Sullins, ICIO; Jerry Johnson, Digital Data System Telemetry/Firing Room Displays; Jack Mueller, LPS Set Support; Mark Greenberg, Saturn Ground Computer Software Support; Richard Mingus, Orbiter Test & Operations Support.

Melbourne, Florida, giving seminars in the evenings, and volunteering in the office during the day. I continued to play tennis and later golf.

Toward the latter part of our marriage I noticed a change in John. He would forget things. In fact, I was the one who had to remember people's names for him. In 2000 I had both knees replaced in one operation. Four weeks later, he told me he didn't love me any more…he was attracted to the massage girl at the fitness club we frequented. His interest wasn't returned as she already had a boyfriend. I couldn't walk very well at the time and this news couldn't have come at a worse time. I was shocked and devastated. I asked him to leave the house and he did. A divorce followed with an agreeable settlement being reached. Several years later he married but that also resulted in divorce.

Many years later he was diagnosed with Alzheimer's and passed away a few months ago.

Since being on my own I have had a very active life. For almost six years I volunteered as a victim's advocate for the State Attorney's Office. I even sang second soprano in my club's chorus. I also became a better Christian Scientist. Today, I write a religious column for my local paper; am on the board for Impact 100, a collective giving organization for women, and also serve on the board of my private club. In the summers I go to my lovely house in the mountains of North Carolina.

Following the Apollo Program, IBM won the Space Shuttle Launch Processing contract, as well as two other key Shuttle systems: Spacelab Integration, with McDonnell-Douglas, and Cargo Integration Test Equipment. A third group at KSC (Shuttle Test & Operations) supported Shuttle launches.

Under the leadership of CEO Louis Gerstner, Jr., the Federal Systems Division of IBM was sold in 1994 to Loral Corporation much to the dismay of NASA and the broken hearts of thousands of IBMers. In 1995, Loral sold its defense electronics and systems integration business to Lockheed Martin. The following year, several of those former Loral units were spun off by Lockheed Martin to become the core of L-3 Communications.

Nothing saddens me more than to hear that some people do not believe we went to the moon. They call it a scam—something born out of a movie studio. Well it wouldn't have taken us 10 years to pull off a movie script in a sound stage. I'm sure that other countries tracked our voyage to the moon, including the Russians who became our partners in Apollo/Soyuz. I'm also sure they would have yelled foul had we been behind a scam.

Yes, I am certain we went to the moon, in fact it was IBM's Instrument Unit that laid out the trajectory, programmed by honest, hard-working IBMers. There were no clandestine meetings, no cover-ups; every meeting was documented and laid down for history. It was honest-to-goodness American ingenuity and hard work that took us to the moon and brought us back safely.

I'm in my 70's as I put the finishing touches on this book and prepare to send it to my publisher. As I look back with gratitude on the many activities and memories of my life, I am always drawn to the wonderful years and people of Apollo. They were special! I Googled many of the people mentioned in this book; most have passed on. I hope I've given you a small glimpse into what it was like for a woman working among all that testosterone of dedicated engineers and astronauts, and everyday people…all committed to a national goal…in those unforgettable years, a time when the IBM banner flew higher, and shone brighter, than it ever had before. It was the time of Apollo, when we all had "The Step."

corsages for the ladies

Jim Bitonti

Apollus Saturnicus genie

....Peace On Earth

....My Country

Scenes from our last Facility Dinner show

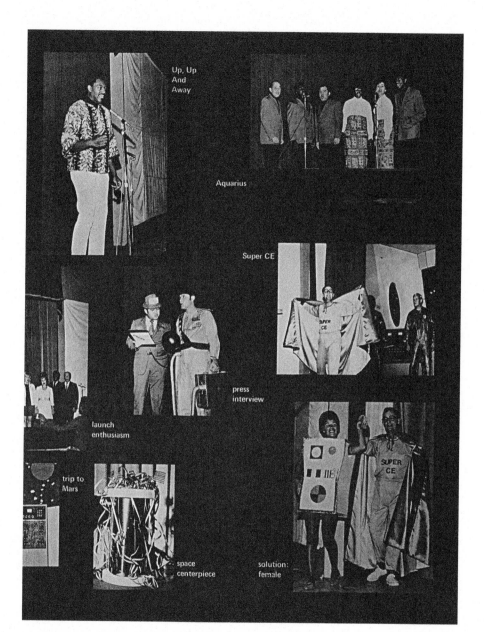

Up, Up
And
Away

Aquarius

Super CE

press
interview

launch
enthusiasm

trip to
Mars

space
centerpiece

solution:
female

ABOUT THE AUTHOR

M artha Goodwin Croskeys Lemasters is a Floridian, reared in Ft. Lauderdale and currently residing in Vero Beach, Florida. During the late 50's, she attended the University of Florida majoring in Journalism.

She began working for IBM at Cape Kennedy as a typist, then secretary and finally PR writer after years of proving herself for advancement. Kennedy Space Center during the difficult 60's was a man's world, made up of engineers, scientists, analysts, programmers and technicians with men outnumbering women 300 to 1. Women were deemed 'safety hazards' if dresses were worn on the launch platforms; disrespect was an everyday occurrence.

As a marketing communications writer, Lemasters wrote about the people who made up one of the greatest technical teams ever assembled in American history. Included in those stories are the heartaches, failures, losses, and challenges to the individuals who made up the Apollo launch support team at the Cape.

Following the end of the Apollo program, she continued into the Skylab and Soyuz programs. After these programs ended she joined Harris Corporation in Melbourne, also as a writer.

Following remarriage in the late 70's to a top executive, she became fully involved as a corporate wife, traveling the world with her husband's ventures into technology, first for the Harris Corporation, then later as president and CEO of CONTEL, which was later bought out by Verizon.

Since retirement, she volunteered for the State Attorney's Office as a victim advocate for six years. During this time, she hosted several concerts for victims entitled *Vero Sings for the Victims.*

Lemasters is a member of Impact 100, a women's collective giving group who each donate $1000 a year and award grants to nonprofits in her community, where she served on the Board as vice president of Communications for five years.

She writes a bi-weekly inspirational article for the Newsweekly section of the Vero Beach Press Journal (tcpalm.com) on behalf of the Christian Science church, where she also serves as a Reader.

She has been a member of the John's Island Club for the past 15 years where she currently serves on the Board of Directors.

RESOURCES

Kennedy Space Center Story, published by National Aeronautics and Space Administration

Apollo – The Race to the Moon by Charles Murray and Catherine Bly Cox

CPSIA information can be obtained at www.ICGtesting.com
Printed in the USA
BVOW08s2154290316

442231BV00002B/2/P